To Jorie—

In the spirit of
caring and sharing.

Best regards,

Carolyn Farb

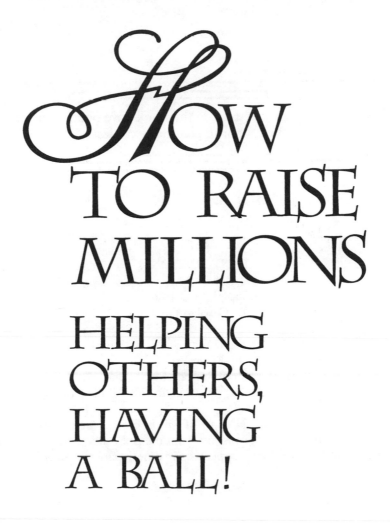

How TO RAISE MILLIONS

HELPING OTHERS, HAVING A BALL!

A GUIDE TO FUNDRAISING

CAROLYN FARB

EAKIN PRESS ★ AUSTIN, TEXAS

A portion of the proceeds from the book have been dedicated
by the author to charitable causes.

FIRST EDITION

Copyright © 1993
By Carolyn Farb

Published in the United States of America
By Eakin Press
An Imprint of Sunbelt Media, Inc.
P.O. Drawer 90159 ★ Austin, TX 78709-0159

ISBN 0-89015-924-6

Library of Congress Cataloging-in-Publication Data

Farb, Carolyn.
  How to raise millions : helping others, having a ball / by Carolyn Farb. — 1st ed.
    p.   cm.
  ISBN 0-89015-924-6 : $22.95
  1. Fund raising — United States. I. Title.
HG177.5.U6F37   1993   93-29479
361.7'0681–dc20   CIP

To Grandpa Jake

for encouraging me to be all that I could be,
and for giving me the courage to dream and the wings to fly.

"Do all the good you can, by all the means you can, in all the ways you can, in all the places you can, at all the times you can, to all the people you can, as long as ever you can."

John Wesley

Contents

Preface   vii

Acknowledgments   ix

Introduction: Jakie's Girl   1

Chapter 1   Putting the Fun in Fundraising   12

Chapter 2   What's In It For Me?   37

Chapter 3   Creative Concepts   57

Chapter 4   Pre-planning   77

Chapter 5   Organization   92

Chapter 6   The Event   106

Chapter 7   Special Touches   117

Chapter 8   Neurofibromatosis:
               The Heart is a Fast Learner   127

Chapter 9   Swine Before Pearls: Jerome's Story   140

Epilogue: Reflections   149

Honors and Awards   151

Fundraising Adventures   153

Index   159

Preface

In the process of writing this book I have become more aware than ever before that the work I do is something I love. It seems the years have flown by; one event has melded into another.

Why do I become involved? Everyone should want to make a difference. The desire to serve is a basic purpose of life. We all are given different gifts and different tasks. I feel strongly that community service is my calling because I come alive when I am in the process of helping someone. Maybe it is the big sister in me or my adventurous spirit. It is a cherished part of my life, my identity, my reason to wake up every day. And it is a permanent part of my life — after twenty years, the art of charity, compassion, and fundraising continues to seduce me, and my passion has not diminished.

It is my hope that the sharing of the experiences in this book and my golden ingredients of fundraising — concept, showmanship/originality, volunteers, budget, commitment, details, decorations, media, delegating, and recognition — will prove helpful to those eager and enthusiastic people who are ready to begin the noble art of fundraising.

Acknowledgments

Fundraising has become an initiative of the American way of pioneering and taking on challenges of worthy social and cultural causes which concern all of us. It takes courage to devote oneself to these causes, but it also takes the willingness of each and every one of us to open our hearts, minds, and checkbooks to support the many fundraising events.

My very special gratitude goes, most of all, to all donors, large and small, who have helped raise the money for so many needy causes. My thanks goes to corporations, foundations, philanthropists, sports associations, and to all my friends — many of them always willing to contribute. My thanks to all donors in kind — restaurants, caterers, retailers, musicians, florists, to name a few — and to the celebrities and artists who have contributed by donating their performances and art in support of my events. I am grateful to the many volunteers who have donated countless hours and services to make it all happen.

I would like to thank the nonprofit organizations, their boards of directors, and their executive directors, who had confidence in me and entrusted me to chair their fundraising campaigns: United Cerebral Palsy, the Stehlin Foundation for Cancer Research, the Texas Neurofibromatosis Foundation at M.D. Anderson Cancer Center, the Challenger Center Gala, the Museum of Fine Arts, Houston, Houston Ballet Foundation, High School for the Performing and Visual Arts, Bering Community Service Foundation, and Volunteers of America, to mention a few. My special thanks to Manny Mones and Bob Hopkins.

And there are many special individuals who have spiritually and physically supported my fundraising and who have encouraged and helped me in bringing this book to you. Their belief in the value of this book inspired me to tell my story. Thanks to my special friend for his guidance and motivation. To my beloved son, Jake Kenyon Shulman, for understanding the importance of my volunteer work and supporting my devotion to my fundraising causes. To my mother, my sister Beverly, and my brother Robert, who have given their ongoing support. Mary Alice Krahl, who taught me the art of communication and the power of a smile. Marilyn Wilhelm, for her enlightened spirit that makes learning a joy. Mickey Herskowitz, for his journalistic expertise and friendship. Lou Congelio, who made the largest contribution of time working through twenty years of personal archives to select the best visuals for the book. Christopher Murray, for his help and advice. Robert Bernstein, for his legal guidance. For their technical assistance and friendship, Kay Murphy and Connie Cooke. And my publisher Ed Eakin, for his belief in the manuscript.

How
TO RAISE
MILLIONS

INTRODUCTION:

Jakie's Girl

Some years ago the late Joe Louis, remembered by many as the greatest of all heavyweight champions, was asked why he had not been more active in the civil rights movement. Louis answered, "Some people do it by marching. Some shout. Some give lots of money. I do it my way. By behaving. All ways count."

My way is to raise as much money as I can for the worthwhile causes in which I believe. I once raised a million dollars in a single night for the Stehlin Foundation for Cancer Research, setting a goal for others to strive to reach.

It should be acknowledged here and now that when you first begin to lend yourself to such efforts, your motives are going to arouse curiosity. That is, until people come to realize this is your calling in life. It is not an ego trip. You are not some kind of dilettante.

There is, of course, an enormous amount of satisfaction to be earned. Call it a sense of accomplishment, of making a contribution. The fact is, the work is there to be done — research programs to be funded, memorials to be built, and services expanded — and in the end knowing what motivates people doesn't matter much. The *doing* is what really matters.

There have been periods in this country when the phrase "do-gooder" began to be regarded with cynicism. I only know that I did

1

not come lately or lightly to this service. What used to be known as charity work is today symbolized in various epic forms. It manifests itself in tribute dinners, fashion luncheons, author/book receptions, celebrity sports events, galas, concerts, telethons, and auctions, to name a few. To me, most of these efforts represent volunteerism in its purest and highest form.

As a teenager, I spent hours after school at Texas Children's Hospital in Houston in the now world-renowned Texas Medical Center, making pimento cheese sandwiches in the snack bar for the patients' families and visitors. At least, in retrospect, those times were much more innocent and less complicated. So were my pimento cheese sandwiches.

I believe that for most of us the idea of caring, of helping the less fortunate, or taking up a cause, grows out of a spirit endowed by someone else along the way. It also comes from deep inside your soul. My own story has a unique quality, a sweet complexity.

My mentor was my beloved grandfather, who was best known as a pioneer Las Vegas hotelman and a high-stakes risk-taker. His name was Jakie Freedman, and he was one of those Napoleon-sized men who tower above their inches.

In the love he lavished on his first grandchild, in the impression he left, he exuded the warmth and charm of a Maurice Chevalier, strutting down the boulevard, twirling his hat, singing "Thank Heaven for Little Girls."

Of course, you would never have caught him in a straw skimmer. He favored ten-gallon hats, cowboy boots, specially designed western clothes, and the memorable fragrance, Tabu. He had an extravagant wardrobe, with close to sixty-five western suits and a hundred hats. I confess I inherited his joie d'vivre, and the fun he enjoyed in being a clotheshorse. I adored his cashmere bathrobes and liked to walk about in them, inhaling the lingering scent of his Tabu.

He called me "Tissue Paper," a teasing but affectionate nickname — a reminder, he said, that precious things come wrapped in tissue paper. He was also aware that I was very sensitive, and he wanted me to learn that in life you have to protect yourself. You can't wear your feelings on your sleeve or you will be disappointed and hurt.

He never drank, but he rolled his own cigarettes. I would be fascinated watching his ritual with the wrappers. He smoked three packs a day, and each time he struck a match he would say to me, "Tissue Paper, I hope you never smoke." And I never have. He had a quality about him that just sparkled. There is no other way to describe it.

Jakie referred to himself as "The Little Man." It was a tradition for him to go to the Kentucky Derby every May, and he enjoyed the pleasure of the gaming tables in casinos owned by his competitors. His nature, his high energy, required a fast-paced life—and he lived it. He owned oil wells, racehorses, and night clubs. He built his "Place in the Sun," The Sands Hotel, on Highway 91. All games of chance except politics fascinated him. He avoided that arena as one would avoid a swamp. "In politics," he said, "the winner will forget you but the loser never does." Jakie had so many Will Rogers-like sayings, funny and wise, that it upsets me that these treasures are not bound in a book to be savored.

Only one with a larger-than-life spirit would boast that people knew him "from Maine to Spain and Nome to Rome." Of course, it wasn't actually a boast if they really knew you, and they knew my grandfather, Jakie Freedman. Even today, people still tell me wonderful Jakie stories.

A Russian immigrant, he was born in Odessa in 1894 and came to this country in his teens, on his own. After World War I, during which he served in the army overseas, he settled in Galveston and sold produce from a cart on a street corner. He used the money he made from the venture to invest in oil, and in the 1920s he struck it rich.

He saved his money and accumulated his wealth, enabling him to join with gusto what he called "the sporting fraternity." He belonged to that inner sanctum of Houston's power brokers that included legendary oilman John Mecom, Sr., Judge James Elkins, and wildcatter Glenn McCarthy. Edna Ferber based both of the main characters in her novel *Giant* on Glenn McCarthy.

On Houston's South Main Street, past the Old Spanish Trail, Jakie built a luxurious mansion with a night club and casino called the Domain Privee. I remember the stately white stone columns reminiscent of the residential area in Houston where I live, known as River Oaks. The private club had its own entrance, and was known for its gourmet food, Hollywood-style entertainment, and a camaraderie that enveloped both the patrons and the staff who worked there and loved Jakie. He had affectionate nicknames for several of his employees. His driver had long sideburns, which prompted Jakie to call him "Mutton Chops."

A driveway lined with palm trees led to the entrance of the main house. The grounds were manicured and landscaped with rose gardens in a classic geometric design. In the coops in back of the main house, chickens laid fresh eggs for breakfast. A marvelous Creole woman named Natalie Petrie, who later went with my grandparents to Las Vegas, was the major-domo of the Domain Privee. My mouth still waters at the thought of her Thanksgiving turkey and Louisiana dirty rice dressing.

The club's fame, and Jakie's, spread throughout the South. Gambling wasn't legal in Texas, but no one seemed to notice — until 1951. With very little fuss, he closed down the club that year.

I still have the china and crystal that belonged to my grandmother, Sadie, when they lived in the big house. It was given to me as a wedding dowry and holds memories I will always treasure of a time gone by. I remember the white chenille carpeting in the formal living room off the black and white marble entry hall, and the wonderful spiral staircase that led to my guest bedroom when I had the special treat of sleeping over.

Jakie loved Houston and Texas, so his next move, to Nevada, was a bittersweet experience. He saw Las Vegas as the new frontier, where gaming was wide open and a town was beginning to blossom in the desert. Once again opportunity beckoned him. He had left his imprint etched into Houston folklore. During the Wall Street crash in 1929, and the bank failures that followed, it was Jakie Freedman who came to the rescue of Houston's First City National Bank, chaired by his good friend, the politically powerful and astute Judge Elkins. While everyone else was taking their money out, my grandfather was putting in all the money he could raise to save the bank and show his faith in his good friend, the Judge. That was one of the many actions that illustrated his strength of character.

I doubt that I could fully explain myself, or my drives, without telling you about my grandfather and my fond memories of Las Vegas. I learned lessons there from a unique perspective about sharing and giving. Does that seem odd, implausible? Las Vegas is a city of big contrasts. But mostly it is a state of mind, where people have always chased their concept of the American dream: the sky is the limit. It is a city of broken hearts and, once, maybe still, of big and tender hearts. My grandfather represented the latter category. He was one of the town's softest touches. No one who came to him for a loan ever went away empty-handed.

He was a close friend of Hank Greenspun, the publisher of the *Las Vegas Sun*, who once wrote of him: "He dug deep into his pockets for a million dollars worth of charity over the past few years. His vices were all minor but his virtues were major – at least $85,000 to clothe poor families in Vegas; setting up people in business; sending an employee's son through law school; stopping on Fremont Street to give enough money to a legless man to buy aluminum legs; and playing gin rummy with a financially busted publisher in the hope, I believe, of losing enough to help the newspaper survive tough times."

I don't believe my grandfather turned his back on anybody. He used to have a saying: "You can't scratch a poor man's back." And whatever his gift, he did it in such a way that he never stripped away anyone's dignity. He taught me the joy of selfless giving.

Greenspun recalled the first time he observed the one-time Russian immigrant, now a jaunty, dapper Texan. He stood before the governor of Nevada and the State Tax Commission, seeking a gambling license, without which his new hotel, to be called The Sands, would be doomed to failure.

"There were some," noted the streetwise newsman, "who would have liked him to be denied." One commissioner was prepared to vote against him because a former applicant who sold out to Jakie had supposedly lied to the commission about a telephone call. Jakie, with the future of a multi-million-dollar investment depending on the good graces of the commission, yelled at them, "What kind of justice do you have in Nevada? Can you deny me a license because someone else lied to you? Catch me in a lie and you cannot only have your license back, but I'll give you each $100,000 to boot. You can never deny Jakie Freedman a license for lying, because he don't lie."

He spoke with an accent, but there was no misunderstanding him. He was a great communicator. No one ever missed his meaning. Before he moved to Las Vegas, from Houston, he was told that he would need to hire a particular Nevada lawyer, a member of the state legislature, if he wanted to get his application approved. Grandpa threw him out of his office with this message: "I'm not applying for a license to practice law. I'm in the gambling business. It's my reputation, not a lawyer's, that the commission will have to consider."

The papers reported that The Sands cost $20 million to build. Jakie Freedman formed a partnership with New York's Jack Entratter, of the famed Copacabana, and the two of them were credited with establishing the glamorous Las Vegas star system.

As a little girl, and even today, I think of him with the reverence reserved for heroes. He was self-made and had originality, wit, compassion and a fierce individuality that is rare. He filled me with awe. It is who we deem heroic that gives us inspiration and vision for tomorrow.

He gambled big, but he also had a prudent streak. He wore around his neck a gold chain with a two-sided medallion, the Star of David on one side and St. Jude on the other. This was a gift from his beloved friend, Danny Thomas. He believed in insurance and wanted to make certain he was covered on both sides of the religious medal. He was not impressed by people with over-inflated egos, but he hit it off instinctively with most entertainers. Danny Thomas was his favorite. He thought of him as a brother. Sammy Davis, Jr., married Mai Britt at The Sands with Frank Sinatra as his best man. Cary Grant was another close family friend, who would take us to dinner whenever he was in Las Vegas. He was dating Dyan Cannon, his future wife, who at the time was singing in the lounge show at The Dunes.

Vegas in the early 1950s was a retreat for Hollywood stars. The legendary gossip columnist Louella Parsons gathered information for her columns while lounging poolside at The Sands with her pal, songwriter Jimmy McHugh. Johnny Mathis, a major heartthrob, was appearing in the Copa Room. Down the street Sophie Tucker, the last of the red hot mamas, was belting out her songs with Ted Mack at the piano at Beldon Katelman's place, El Rancho Vegas. The Flamingo featured the big band of Harry James. One could see Betty Grable sitting on a bar stool listening to his sounds. There were wall-to-wall stars, producers, agents, and their fans, the people who have always been on the fringe watching Hollywood types, wanting the glitter to rub off.

The Strip was the exclusive place to be in those days. Downtown, at the Horseshoe and the Fremont hotels, serious sportin' men gambled with cash. Howard Hughes was becoming visible in Vegas, not yet a victim of his own paranoia. Private planes would land at

McCarran Field, and private cars bounded across the tarmac to meet the passengers at the foot of the landing stairs. The hospitality and charm of a small town prevailed and welcomed everyone. The only hospital was run by an order of nuns. The population for the area generally surrounding the Resort Area of Las Vegas Boulevard, also known as the Las Vegas Strip, was 24,000 in 1960. In 1992, the population of the area from downtown to the airport was 80,161. Caesar's Palace, the Stardust, and the Frontier had yet to be built, but the place already had the feel of a fantasy land: flashing neon in the middle of a sandpile surrounded by mountains.

I have never gambled, but I can appreciate the excitement once it gets under your skin. It's easy to get caught up in the sound and color of it. Personalities become redefined in this never-never land. People bet on which way an elevator is going.

It was at the Horseshoe Casino one night that my grandfather played in a dice game that became a part of Vegas folklore. A million dollars changed hands. At one point, he said, he was down by $500,000, but he rallied and eventually walked away with a loss of only $30,000.

The casino was strictly off-limits to me on my vacations. I was instructed to walk quickly through the casino, preferably around the perimeter, never stopping. My grandmother, Sadie, taught me to play gin, and I feel fairly confident about my game. But mostly I enjoyed the private time I spent with Grandma Sadie, who was actually my step-grandmother. She always looked like a movie star when they attended the glamorous hotel openings. I loved watching her "dressing up" ritual. She was an elegant woman with jet-black hair who resembled the Duchess of Windsor, and she had the most beautiful hands and alabaster skin I have ever seen. She would take me with her when she would go to Beverly Hills to shop for the fall season. As it was still a small town in the desert, Las Vegas had limited shopping in those days.

Like Jakie, she loved the horses, and after he died she maintained a suite in the hotel's Belmont Park. The wings of the hotel were all named after his favorite racetracks around the country. My grandfather once named a thoroughbred after me, Carolyn F., and one for my brother, Robert. Mine, regrettably, was always getting scratched.

It is difficult, if not impossible, to write about someone you

adored without romanticizing them. You try to recall every memory
to do them justice. But I don't think the times have fooled me. The
Freedman kids were blessed with a special legacy, and as the first-
born I was the twinkle in Jakie's eye. I remember I was such a skinny
kid that he would pay me a dollar to drink a malt and five dollars for
a malt with an egg in it. I was willing to be bribed; however, the malts
were filling, and I could never put away enough of them to build up
any serious cash reserves. I'm not sure why or how, but that setting
influenced me in an unexpected way. My grandfather's generous way
of helping others was an early inspiration and example which influenced my commitment to fundraising and serving others.

To keep me busy during my summer vacations, Jakie gave me a
job in his office. He put me to work with Louise Maxwell, his loyal
executive secretary, organizing his scrapbooks. He referred to her as
his "brood mare" and I was forever "the filly." Max was like a member of our family and I was like a member of hers. Together we did
the normal things that native Las Vegans did, such as taking excursions to the Hoover Dam with Max's family, and going to the movies
and restaurants off the Strip.

Being a child, I had to balance the life of growing up with my
family in West University Place, a friendly and charming neighborhood in Houston near Rice Institute, and what became the magical
experiences of traveling west on the train to visit my grandparents in
Nevada during vacations. Those were fantasy times, and I always remembered the words of my mother not to talk to strangers and to
keep my money tucked safely in my cowboy boot. After getting off
the train in Las Vegas, we went straight to The Sands for an immediate hot fudge sundae fix in the Garden Room. During my visits to
Las Vegas, we would sometimes travel to Los Angeles for his business meetings. What youngster would not have been thrilled to be on
the motion picture studio lots at Columbia and Metro Goldwyn
Mayer, and be invited into the inner sanctums of the grand movie
moguls?

My grandfather knew the famous studio heads, Harry Cohn of
Columbia Pictures and Joe Pasternak of MGM Studios, and we were
given the royal treatment. I daydreamed about becoming an actress
and avidly collected autographed pictures of movie stars. One day
Mr. Cohn arranged for a makeup artist to "do" my face, and Grandpa
and I had our photographs taken at Columbia. I still remember think-

ing how awful I looked.

My eyes used to drink in all the glamorous, exciting, awesome things evolving around me as I sat in the studio commissary. Part of my excitement was in knowing the pleasure my grandfather took in my reactions. I always tried to live up to his expectations. He wanted the best for me and from me. He didn't want the status quo. I knew this inherently. He wanted me to set an example, be above reproach, reach for the moon and the stars. These were romantic and powerful thoughts for a young girl, but they set me apart as a child. He made me want to aspire.

The Sands kept a reservations office next door to the historic Beverly Wilshire Hotel, where my grandfather's picture hung on the wall. I recall our lunching across the street at the Brown Derby with his friends, the singer Tony Martin and his actress wife, Cyd Charisse. Grandpa Jake adored Cyd's legs, as did many others.

He would arrange for his friends to take me to the Farmer's Market and go shopping at Lanz Originals for clothes. At that time, Lanz was the rage with my contemporaries.

He was as generous with himself and his time as he was with his resources. Most mornings we would breakfast together at the bungalow on Sadie Lane, named after my grandmother, and listen to the radio soap operas. "Stella Dallas" was his all-time favorite. I was vaguely aware that someone of importance leased the bungalow behind ours. When Howard Hughes was in town, his food would be delivered to him in an ambulance. I would have spied on him if I had only realized who he was and how legendary his eccentricities would become. Instead, I was busy with my Brownie camera, photographing the local desert vegetation.

Grandpa Jake used to ride in the El Dorado parade in Palm Springs with Ray Ryan, owner of the El Mirador, with his friend Gene Autry and other celebrated cowboys. We had matching western outfits. A wonderful bootmaker from Amarillo would come to us twice a year to measure us for these special boots.

When I was in college at the University of Oklahoma, Jakie died. I was devastated. After a New Year's party at the hotel, he complained that his hand was hurting, the result, he thought, of greeting so many people. He was misdiagnosed by a famous eastern clinic as having rheumatoid arthritis. The reality was that he needed to have bypass surgery and would likely have lived years longer had the problem been diagnosed correctly. In retrospect, he should have stopped long enough to let his good friend, Dr. Denton Cooley, perform the cardiovascular surgery that surely would have saved his life.

The strain on his heart soon took its toll. In January of 1958 he was flown to Los Angeles and was admitted to Mount Sinai Hospital. On January 19 he died on the operating table. The doctors said later that his heart had stopped eight times.

When Grandpa died, the saddest day of my life, there was one western outfit he had never worn. It was black trimmed with silver leather. The shirt was silver metallic with a matching fabric belt and a great western buckle. My mother took me to a tailor and had the suit remade for me. It meant so much because I knew how he loved wearing his western clothes, and wearing that last outfit made me feel close to him.

A memorial service was held in Los Angeles, and he was buried in the family plot in Houston. He was sixty-four, and had so much more living to do. The night he died, the lights on the Strip blinked off, the hotels went dark, and gambling stopped for a while in tribute to Jakie Freedman. No one could recall such a tribute having been paid before, and it would not happen again until April of 1976, the night Howard Hughes died.

It is true, I think, that the qualities that shape our character often skip a generation. I know Jakie's spirit is inside me. For many, college and marriage smooth off the edges and lend a layer of social polish. It didn't happen that way for me. I had an earlier start than most. Jakie and Sadie Freedman gave me an interest in a wide range of people. They taught me to be willing to give. I was a keen observer with Las Vegas as my window, and I learned. To quote Yogi Berra, "You can observe a lot just by watching."

Any ardent gambler will tell you that the key to winning isn't luck or nerve. It is management. It is how you manage your finances, time, and distractions. Nothing encourages concentration quite as much as having all your chips on the line.

These were among the lessons that made up the approach I wanted to bring to my charitable planning.

In the 1970s I returned to Las Vegas for a tribute to Joe Louis, who in the final years of his life worked as a greeter at Caesar's Palace. A larger than life-sized, white marble statue of the great champion adorned the entry to the Olympia wing of the hotel.

The city and the elaborate hotels were still dazzling, but I hoped it would be the way it was when Grandpa was there. I wanted to stop at the bellman's desk and see if Red Viens, once a skating partner of Sonja Henie, and all the people I knew as a kid were still there; to check out the snack bar and see if Shirley, the pretty Eurasian woman who made the greatest hot fudge sundaes ever, was still behind the counter; to stop by and say hello to Dorothy Beal, who owned the very exclusive hotel dress shop where my grandfather used to pick out my special surprises. My first sense of fashion and what I perceived as glamour probably came from that exposure. Within this never-never-land background, there were always rules and disciplines.

In Las Vegas today, they keep building bigger and more extravagant hotels. But something is missing. I think it is "The Little Man's" heart.

CHAPTER 1

Putting the Fun in Fundraising

$\mathbf{M}$any people believe and, indeed, live by the adage that no good deed goes unpunished. I disagree with that.

I feel good about saying that I am proud of what I do, what John D. Rockefeller once described as "the business of benevolence." I have always likened such work to a calling. The late Miss Nina Cullinan, a Texaco heiress, patroness of the arts and one of my heroines, referred to this quality as a gift.

Today there are many more causes than there are people and organizations willing to initiate fundraisers. Charity in America, in the 1990s, is a billion-dollar-a-year industry. While there is a big effort to reach deep into the population for funds, there is very little understanding of the mechanics to do so. Distinctions should be made between appeals that range from luncheons, auctions, and telethons to the big, high-priced celebrity galas. On the surface, it appears glamorous when you read the newspaper coverage of the gala event; however, in reality the event has been preceded by months of hard work and creative planning, in addition to great teamwork and fun.

There is no such thing as a short history of fundraising, but a few basic facts of introduction might be helpful. Philanthropy is not a word one hears as often today as fifty years ago. The practice didn't begin in this country, but Americans gave it scale and a personal flair. The original Rockefeller, John D., is best remembered for giving away dimes to strangers during the Depression. He started with nickels but found them too heavy. Yet, according to the *Guiness Book of Records,* in his lifetime he gave away $750 million.

Andrew Carnegie came to America in 1835 as a poor immigrant, the son of a Scotsman, and made a fortune in the steel industry. At fifty-four, he decided to start giving away his wealth, which by 1901 was valued at $492 million. It was Carnegie who advanced the theory in this country that charity was not so much a religious duty as a social obligation.

Whatever one thought of the motives or morals of the Rockefellers, the Carnegies, and the so-called "robber barons" of their time, the money they gave came out of their own pockets. Tax deductions were not allowed for charitable gifts until 1917.

There is a revealing story told about John D. Rockefeller, while he and his wife were touring Ireland. A priest persuaded him to donate $5,000 to a Catholic home for wayward boys. The next day, the American tycoon opened a Dublin newspaper to find a glaring headline: "Rockefeller Gives $50,000 to Saint Thomas Home." Livid, Rockefeller summoned the priest and gave him a tongue lashing. Yet, at the same time, he realized he could not recant a gift for which he was now being commended in print. Finally, he agreed to contribute the extra $45,000 on the condition that he be allowed to write the inscription over the entrance once the home was completed. At the dedication ceremonies, curiosity was at a fever pitch as Rockefeller stepped forward to pull the string to remove the drape covering his dedication. It read: "I was hungry and you fed me. I was naked and you clothed me. I came as a stranger and you took me."

As a personal matter, I have never felt the need to look too closely into why people give. I would rather applaud the fact that they do give.

A poll conducted by the market research firm of Daniel Yankelovich found that donors who were polled gave, or said they did, for three basic reasons. Sixty percent said they gave out of a sense of moral obligation, slightly more than a third said their motivation was the satisfaction of helping others, and a handful (two percent) said they gave out of guilt. As the saying goes, it doesn't matter how you load the truck, as long as it gets loaded.

From the start, you know you will need to negotiate with a wide variety of people, some of whom will make commitments and then waver. I operate on the basis of a handshake. This I learned from my grandfather, Jake, that a man's word is his bond, or should be. It is the approach I prefer, even though it heightens the element of risk and there is no safety net.

Another policy of mine is to get every possible expense underwritten. The goal is to make certain that the worthwhile and needy cause, and/or the organization, receives the total contribution. It is disappointing when those who organize or chair a nonprofit event lose their focus and compromise these goals.

Once a restauranteur agreed to underwrite the cost of a pre-party event. As the time drew near, he had second thoughts and asked what our budget was. Of course, he knew we had no budget and were counting on him. This had been made clear to him in the beginning when I expressed to him how valuable the exposure would be for his business. He was waffling, and I had to stand firm. This is not unlike corporate negotiating. The executive director of the non-profit group, myself, and the restauranteur had a meeting that began in a cold war atmosphere. But after recalling our initial conversation and his commitment to the project, he kept his word.

If one wants to be a fundraiser, one has to be flexible. There are not many role models in the field. You have to be willing to trailblaze. There are no job promotions or retirement plans. The buck stops with you. You can't pass responsibilities over to someone else. The work is hard and at times can be thankless.

Fundraising requires a concentrated effort involving imagination, hard work, and a keen business sense. If you can only remember one of these, stick with hard work. It is consuming, uplifting, and personally rewarding.

I intend this book to be a celebration of the art of sharing and giving. But one should know that obstacles occur.

In planning an event, I try to give the best I can. I always pose the question to myself: "What is the most people-considerate thing I can offer?" Today there are so many functions for a multiplicity of worthwhile causes that people suffer burnout and become wary of being involved at all. They feel as though they are on a treadmill going nowhere. An event has to be thought out in such a way that, psychologically, you can tap into the comfort zones we all have. You have to offer something in your scheme that will register a home run.

Fundraising, for me, is having a full-time job for which you don't get paid. This surprises the people who might assume I receive a fee or a percentage of the funds raised. There are fundraising consulting firms who charge a fee based on services or a percentage based on the amount of funding raised.

Fundraising has become a rapidly growing industry. I have been doing this on a voluntary basis for at least twenty years, and I have been asked about founding a school on this subject. There is a need for such knowledge. In this book I will share mine, beginning with my ten-point formula.

Concept

My formula for fundraising has evolved over a number of years, and it always begins with *concept*. To be a fundraiser, it helps to be a visionary. Every concept must be the right fit into the overall scheme. Your first priority is to set a realistic goal. Fundraising offers a challenge and a fresh set of circumstances every time you undertake a new project. There is an excitement that I get when my head begins to fill with creative ideas. I try to envision the results these dreams might accomplish. It is always beneficial to be able to draw from your past projects and experiences. Let me tell you about some of mine.

The Challenger Center benefit concert was dedicated to establishing educational centers in memory of the *Challenger* crew who perished. Instead of one learning center, the families envisioned a network of facilities that simulate what it would be like to live and work in space. The affiliate Challenger Centers could be added to existing museum and public school buildings. "To be a progressive America, we must have an ambitious pioneer spirit that takes us into the future," June Scobee said. The *Challenger* tragedy left behind grieving families and a haunted nation. Our dream concert was an opportunity to channel those painful emotions into a positive, healing legacy for the nation as well as the family members.

The *Challenger* families felt that a well-coordinated press conference at the Museum of Natural Science, where the Challenger Learning Center was to be located, would be the best site to announce the chairman and other pertinent details of the upcoming concert. We invited both print and air media to the museum. June Scobee presented me with a pair of her husband's flight gloves, and Jane Smith gave me a "magical" wand to lead us on a successful mission. We announced to the press that a benefit concert would be held on March 31, 1988, with Brooke Shields, Melba Moore, Pia Zadora, Gary Morris, and the Fabulous Thunderbirds to raise the funds for the first of many learning centers to be opened across the nation. The honorary chairs for the gala were Vice President and Mrs. George Bush.

Our goal with the Stehlin Foundation was to raise $1 million in one evening to support needed cancer research. The concept for the event grew out of a reception held in my home for the Houston Pops Orchestra. Among the guests that evening were Dr. John Stehlin, a leading cancer oncologist and founder of the Stehlin Foundation for Cancer Research, and the special guest of honor, Marvin Hamlisch, whose mother had recently died of cancer.

That night, Marvin and I agreed to co-host a gala concert to benefit and to raise the $1 million needed for Dr. Stehlin's ongoing research programs. Our lineup of stars included Liza Minnelli, Ann Margret, Alan King, Crystal Gayle and, of course, the talented and amiable Hamlisch. We had our concept and we had our million-dollar goal. This is where you begin.

Our next step was to set a date. It is important that the date of the event not conflict with that of another major organization. Also, a location has to be determined. The seating capacity of the facility determines the price structuring relative to the targeted goal. We had to offer different levels of ticket prices for a variety of supporters. We chose Jones Hall, a 3,000-seat performing arts hall which would be a challenge to fill. We allocated certain rows at $50, in consideration of those Stehlin supporters who could not afford the higher ticket prices.

The University of Houston athletic director, Rudy Davalos, asked me to chair a fundraiser which we decided to call "A Tribute to Excellence." It appealed to me because of the commitment all great athletes have to excellence and self-discipline. Two of the world's greatest athletes, Olympian Carl Lewis and Houston Rocket All-Star Hakeem Olajuwon, were honored at the exciting inaugural Tribute to Excellence. Lewis at the time had won six national collegiate championships at the University of Houston. He won four medals at the 1984 Olympics, two more in 1988, and would add his seventh and eighth in 1992 in Barcelona. Olajuwon, an All American center for the Cougars, led the University of Houston to three straight appearances in the NCAA Final Four including two championship games. He would go on to establish himself as one of the premier centers in the NBA with the Houston Rockets.

The coup was in finding a member of a private country club, where we wanted to hold the event, to sponsor the University of Houston tribute dinner honoring two black athletes. In your role as a fundraising volunteer, remember you can take steps to change and improve the world through your visionary deeds. Hopefully, you will change the perspective in the process. Choosing to go out on a limb can be risky. However, I strongly believe in the edict of no risk, no gain. You will not be alone for long.

For the cover of our invitation I envisioned Hakeem and Carl in their U of H letter sweaters with Hofheinz Pavilion in the background. Who wouldn't want to support the first presentation of these scholar athletic awards named for local Houston philanthropists Mary G. Cullen and Lucile Melcher? There was an incredibly short time frame and an August date, both inherent obstacles to overcome. Another factor in selecting a mutually convenient date was the athletes' busy schedules.

We did a mailing of 5,000 invitations, but I have found through experience you should never rely on mail responses alone. That is one risk I will never take. I literally sold out the event by phone and fax machine. You must leave as little as possible to chance, especially when you realize others are depending on you. The personal touch always makes the difference. It is the bottom line – the difference between success and failure. Remember that competition is tight for the charity dollar, and as our economy fluctuates it will become even tighter. It is easy to throw an invitation into the infamous File 13, but very hard to say no to someone making a direct contact. Sometimes the mail never reaches the person for whom it is intended. It can be blocked by a well-intending and overly protective secretary. You must not be discouraged. I draw strength and courage from my own personal mantra by remembering that I am asking for funding not for myself, but for an organization I am firmly committed to.

My idea was to showcase the University of Houston and its many natural resources and assets. We used their pep rally groups, the Buggy Beauties and the Cougar Dolls. The pre-party event was catered by the University of Houston Conrad Hilton Inn, College of Hotel and Restaurant Management Par Excellence campus food services. In keeping with the spirit of the night, Southwest Conference and NCAA Championship trophies adorned each table as center-pieces. Messages from President George Bush, CBS's Jim Nantz (a University of Houston graduate), and NBA Commissioner David Stern, as well as career highlights, were presented on video. It was very impressive to walk into the ballroom at the country club where the event was held and see just how many championship trophies the University of Houston Athletic Department had been awarded. The point was well taken. I wanted people to experience that old college try. And they did. Coincidentally, that year the University of Houston produced a Heisman Trophy winner in Andre Ware.

The former University of Houston basketball coach, Guy Lewis, and University of Houston patron, Mrs. Leroy Melcher, made the presentation to Hakeem Olajuwon. Cougar track coach Tom Tellez, along with Mrs. Roy Cullen, presented Carl Lewis his award.

All of the guests received souvenir T-shirts underwritten by the law firm of Norton & Blair. Coming up with the design for the shirt was part of the creative fun. Neiman Marcus contributed Baccarat crystal #1's to the Gold table hosts. Our $7,500 Gold underwriter table sponsors were invited to a pre-reception with the honorees, were recognized in the program, and received the underwriter's gift and a photo opportunity with Carl and Hakeem. The $5,000 Silver table sponsors were invited to the reception, received special recog-nition in the program, and were given eight tickets to a University of Houston athletic event of choice and a gift of a small silver box. The $2,500 Bronze patron tables received special recognition and four tickets to a University of Houston athletic event of choice. Special guests in the audience included Olympian Mary Lou Retton, former Houston Rockets coach Don Chaney, present Rockets coach Rudy Tomjohnavich, and Rockets owner Charlie Thomas and his wife, Kittsie.

Showmanship

After formulating the concept, the next stage is *showmanship*. This has to do with the presentation of an event. At the Challenger Center benefit concert, I wanted our supporters to *feel* why they were there. In the grand foyer of the Wortham Center, I commemorated our fallen heroes with American flags symbolizing each member of the crew that perished. The flags were the first visuals that people saw as they stepped off the escalator, which set the patriotic mood for the entire evening. Clearly, this was one of those exceptional cases where every touch, every nuance, every subtlety had to be done with utmost sensitivity and heartfelt patriotism.

It is always important to give your event that spark of originality. The guests were delighted by the appearance of a group of urban roller skaters in futuristic space costumes, gliding across the grand foyer of the Wortham Center. Frankel's Costume Co., Inc., provided the costumes for the skaters. Originally, we had planned for them to skate around a missile on loan from NASA in front of the Wortham Center, but inclement weather had forced us to move inside. The move provided the right balance of whimsy and fantasy. Nothing was lost because of the flexibility and positive team spirit everyone should have when a problem occurs.

Showmanship allows our imagination to soar and brings out the Cecil B. De Mille in each of us. For example, at the Museum of Fine Arts "A Renaissance Evening," food service people were dressed in Renaissance costumes to enhance the decorative theme, and guests were greeted by jugglers and fire eaters and entertained by tarot card readers, face painters, and belly dancers.

At the United Cerebral Palsy Starathon '90, I scheduled the Goodyear Blimp to hover over The Galleria, where the telethon was held, and it blinked a starry night message of good wishes.

The Business Arts Fund, founded in 1974, is an organization through which corporations support the city's major cultural groups with a single contribution. Since its inception, this group has given $12 million to its affiliates. Some of the cultural art affiliates are the Alley Theater, Contemporary Arts Museum, Theater Under the Stars, and the Harris County Heritage Society, to name a few.

The Folie du Ciel "Sky Follies" was an event organized by the Business Arts Fund to thank the corporate executives and their families. An awards presentation was staged during the outing to recognize companies that had contributed significantly to the affiliate nonprofit organizations. The event was a catered picnic, exhibition polo match by the Houston Polo Team, and an afternoon of jazz music. As a special thank you to the corporate donors, they were invited to board a regatta of hot air balloons after the polo match at the Bayou

Club. The grand finale was the lifting off of ten hot air balloons – and what a majestic sight it was.

Walking canes were a popular party favor in keeping with a Southern theme for the "Soiree on the Swanee" Ballet Ball. Such favors help to create the right ambiance for your benefactors and to give them a memory that will linger.

Volunteers

The next major phase of fundraising is to organize the *volunteers*. It is said that wars are won not by the armies you have but by the armies your enemy thinks you have. Without volunteers and donors, our budgets would be nonexistent. Once a nonprofit organization has benefited from the talent and energy of a volunteer, especially a chairperson, that volunteer needs to be recognized and remembered in a significant way. If a chairperson has established an event that will be ongoing for your organization, that person should be remembered as a founder who initiated a valuable and valid method for raising funds for the cause. The chairperson will feel good about contributing that part of his or her life to your organization.

Strokes are nurturing not only to your donors but to your volunteers as well. Even the volunteer who feels that his or her contribution was modest is still deserving of a thank you. Remember, this is a gift of self that should be accepted graciously.

Volunteers are the loyal soldiers who place the programs, menus, favors, and centerpieces on tables. Volunteers perform the magic. They work at the reservation desk, collect funds, check people in, and direct people to their tables. Volunteers address envelopes and ultimately parcel them off to the post office.

Updating a mailing list is an ongoing job for a persevering volunteer. This can be done on a monthly basis. Additionally, volunteers can redirect returned mail, and with the help of a friendly computer, maintain the lists.

Mailing lists are notoriously obsolete almost as soon as your mailing is completed. People divorce, move, their forwarding addresses expire, or they change companies. This makes it almost impossible to keep the mailing list current. No matter how extensive your mailing list is, someone is always not included. You must ask yourself, who am I not reaching? This is when you have to do some hands-on networking. Volunteers can make a person-to-person telephone push, canvassing friends and associates to buy tickets. The main objective when you are having an event is to have people attend as well as buy the tickets. You want a good turnout. If supporters can't use their tickets, encourage them to give them to friends. They can turn tickets or table reservations back to the chairperson to resell or fill tables with deserving campaign volunteers who may be unable to afford tickets.

Volunteers distribute posters and place them in high-traffic locations such as shopping malls, downtown tunnel systems, grocery stores, and movie theaters. A well-articulated poster can take the place of an invitation in a given situation. Volunteers help decorate, break down after an event, and return any loaned items to florists, designers, and retailers.

Every individual involved is important to the overall success of a fundraising event. People have limitations on their time, so encourage your volunteers to make their own decisions about the area they can best serve. Remember your volunteers are people with personal needs and their own busy schedules. You should value their opinions and recognize their contributions. At a meeting or function, honor them with a round of applause. Highlight their achievements in press releases and on other occasions when there is media coverage. Plan work sessions in comfortable surroundings. If some of the work is done after dark, be certain that you provide security to see them to their cars. If the organization you are serving has a newsletter, recognize volunteers and encourage their input for the team planning. Be certain that they are familiar with the nonprofit agency and goals that are set for the specific event. Volunteers should be given the opportunity to work on the committee of their choice for a gala or fundraising luncheon. Committee categories might include invitations, menus, reservations, individual ticket and table sales, decorations, publicity, and clean-up.

A volunteer network can accomplish the impossible. This is illustrated by the Houston Public Television Auction that was held annually for twenty years. Jim Bauer, the former general manager of KUHT Public Television, recalled the hoopla of the auction. In the early days, the Channel 8 auction was responsible for attracting people and helping them to become aware of public television. Of course, the money that was raised was vital to keeping the station on the air, as the programming in those days was limited. In later years, the amount that was raised by the auction in respect to the overall budget decreased as the membership grew. In the beginning days, forty percent of the overall revenue was provided by the auction. You might say the auction launched the station. This was before the days of cable, and there were only three local stations. Channel 8 was on the bottom of the dial, and if not for the auction hoopla, no one would have tuned in.

In an event such as this, volunteers collect auction items by canvassing the city. Items range in value from $50 into the thousands. The volunteers categorize and identify the items to be auctioned. During the telethon they handle the phones, verify the bids, organize the "pick-up and pay," and deliver the items if they are not picked up at the station. They operate the hospitality and food tents with a smile and provide good cheer during the auction.

Some of the most fun that I can remember was when I served as chairperson of the Channel 8 Auction Super Sports Night in 1973. We raised $252,264. I wanted to do something that would create an air of excitement for that particular evening.

Even in the early 1970s, before sports became such a high-profile event, I realized the value of involving athletes in support of worthwhile nonprofit organizations. The emphasis today has moved from Hollywood box-office stars to the hero worship of athletes. Not only did we have an array of specially autographed basketballs, tennis rackets and golf clubs, but these high-profile sports celebrities agreed to do the auctioning. I had the fun of meeting Polish wrestler Ivan Putski and even putting him in a hammer lock. Although Ivan doesn't lay claim to the World of Wrestling lore, his promoters said he was the strongest guy on the grunt and groan circuit, the type that could crush concrete blocks with his bare hands.

Robert Mosbacher, a Houston oilman and former secretary of commerce, donned his yachting togs. Neiman Marcus retailer Lawrence Marcus was there in chic polo attire to help with the auctioning. The Oilers' Kenny Houston, hockey's John Schella, baseball's Leo Durocher, and Solly Hemus of the old Houston Buffs baseball team all became a part of this unique group of sports personalities I was able to enlist for that evening. It became the "in" place to be. There was good fellowship in the holding room before each group went on for their shift.

In 1987, at the "Evening of Hope" benefit to establish an AIDS dental clinic and provide funding for AIDS research, there was a physical need for manpower. Artworks of all sizes had to be transported after the intermission from the lobby of Houston's Alley Theater to Jones Plaza directly across the street. The art would be auctioned later in the evening on Jones Plaza at the post-gala celebration. This was accomplished by our volunteers, who had also handled the installation of the art at the theater.

Volunteerism will keep people active and visible, and will provide potential career opportunities through networking. It is a great meeting forum to exchange creative ideas and values. The networking and interacting when volunteering can be very appealing and is one of the major pluses of fundraising for those who choose to become involved. An acquaintance, Annette Strauss, for many years dedicated herself to serving as a volunteer, then went on to convert her talents into associating with an advertising and public relations firm. From there she became mayor of Dallas.

Budget

Your supporters deserve to know that their money is going directly to the cause. This is an unwritten, unspoken bond that must exist between you and them. It would be easy to work with an unlimited budget. I always operate on the premise that we are working from a *zero* budget, which calls for great ingenuity and management.

At a fundraiser for the Rice Design Alliance called "A Step Back In Time," I used antique toys as the focal point of our table centerpiece design. This was an original and practical idea as well as thematic. I met an antique dealer quite by chance at Mrs. Fields Cookie Shop, and through her a proposal was made to a co-op of antique dealers to participate in the evening. In keeping with our theme of the anniversary celebration of the organization and having zero funding, I thought that antique toys would be interesting as well as conversational centerpieces.

The antique association loaned us the toys, and at the same time they had the opportunity to broaden their client base. We built our table design around these charming toys, complemented by lace overlays and native magnolia leaves and flowers. Even the fabric for the tables had been purchased at a bargain outlet and hemmed by our volunteer group.

Once the concept had been decided upon, everything fell into place. For the auction items, I had asked well-known architects, designers, and artists, who made up the majority of the Rice Design Alliance membership, to design and create toys in conjunction with the twentieth anniversary of the Alliance. The event also honored the retiring dean of the Rice Architectural School, O. Jack Mitchell.

A big thrill for me is to succeed on the zero-budget plan. Again, I consider this part of the unwritten contract with contributors. No donor or patron wants large portions of the funds they donate to pay for administrative costs or decorative frills. They want to know that their money is going to directly address a specific need.

The pre-event for the second annual Texas Neurofibromatosis Foundation fundraiser was scheduled to be held at Dave and Buster's. I didn't know what a Dave and Buster's was when Dave first contacted me. This very dynamic young entrepreneur came up to me during a reception and wanted to talk about being involved with one of my fundraising projects in the future.

A year later, I thought I'd call him and see if he was still interested in offering support. His corporate office is located in Dallas. We set up a meeting in Houston at Dave and Buster's with his partner, Buster, and their marketing and public relations representatives.

When I arrived at the place, I had no idea what to expect or suggest. First of all, it is 52,000 square feet. I immediately liked their concept. Dave gave me the tour before lunch. Usually you can't get near their parking lot, so I was thinking to myself that perhaps my timing in accepting his generous offer might be a year too late.

We passed the pocket billiard area, the play-for-fun blackjack casino, the putting green, bowling alley, the Million Dollar Midway and the D&B Bop, and my eyes continued to be amazed. I had landed in the middle of an adult play park.

They agreed to host the pre-event for the NF Benefit "I've Got A Crush On You," which would acknowledge the honorees, underwriters, and special friends. We agreed that we would limit the guests to 200 people. The Neurofibromatosis Foundation would prepare the invitation, which would be submitted for their approval. We would handle the invitation mailing, responses, and name tags. Our guests would have the total Dave and Buster's experience. They would gather in the '50s D&B Bop for lavish hors d'oeuvres, open bar, program and dancing, then venture out to enjoy the fun of the midway.

I knew most of the attendees probably had never been to this unique place and would have a fun experience.

A major responsibility of mine and anyone at the helm is to get everything donated or underwritten. I never waver in my belief that there are individuals and corporations wanting to become involved if they are only given the chance to participate. This means *never being afraid to ask.* The adage "Nothing ventured, nothing gained" certainly holds true.

In 1979, when I was chairing "The Soiree on the Swanee" to benefit the Houston Ballet Foundation, I had noticed fashion designer Bill Blass was introducing a line of bed linens that reflected our Southern theme. He donated the sheets, lavender nasturtium on a creme background, which our volunteers in charge of decorations sewed into overlays for the skirted tables.

When you are involved in a project, you have to be receptive to all types of information because you never know when it will be helpful to you. You might find that you want to store it in your own personal idea database for a future date. This creative idea worked well as it involved an American fashion designer with a local project. Many of the women attending the ball would be wearing his designs, so he was happy to support our effort on behalf of the Houston Ballet in giving to community enrichment.

Bill even helped with some of our pre-ball press. In an effort to build up momentum for the upcoming ball, Bill and I dressed black-tie and found ourselves on a float in my pool in the middle of winter amidst oversized pampas grass and white swans. Fearing he would fall in and catch a cold, I turned on the pool heater. It created the most dreamy, steamy photograph one can imagine.

When high-ticket sales appear soft or not moving as quickly as you would like, offer incentives to high-ticket prospects. With the "Evening of Hope" AIDS fundraiser, we gave our prospective benefactors the opportunity to attend a brunch with actress Piper Laurie, who was starring in the Alley Theater's production of *The Last Flapper.* Another incentive for sponsors was a framed lithograph by artists Jack Boynton and Trudy Sween.These are measures that can help bolster ticket sales with a first event or when there is no built-in support group.

California-based couture designer James Galanos donated one of his original gowns to the United Cerebral Palsy Starathon '90 Telethon. We would not have been able to purchase such a gown that retails for $7,500. Galanos' donation added a glamorous dimension to the auction and helped us reach our grand total of $650,000. This was only the third telethon held in Houston on behalf of United Cerebral Palsy, and we placed second in the nation.

As you can imagine, fashion designers and retailers are often besieged with requests, and they do what they can to support as many causes as possible. Depending on their year and other economic factors, they may or may not decide to participate, but it is always worth your effort to try.

Chili's, a franchise chain headquartered in Dallas, fed our 700 volunteers from Friday until the telethon ended on Sunday. This represented an in-kind donation of $7,000 on the part of Chili's. With donations from Chili's and other in-kind donors, we were able to operate on my zero-budget philosophy. It is always nice when there are no strings attached.

I met with officials from Hyundai of America and their local dealers and assured them that goodwill and community exposure could be as effective as paid advertising. They donated a Hyundai Sonata valued at $15,000. If there wasn't a comparable bid, they were prepared to bid on the car at $15,000. Fortunately, an even higher bid was placed.

Of course, you can't just woo donors with empty words. Foley's included the Hyundai Sonata in the nationally established annual Thanksgiving Day Parade, which assured the kind of visibility I had hoped to deliver. Several of the United Cerebral Palsy poster representatives rode in the car, which was adorned with a UCP banner. I arranged for the car to be on display at The Galleria for two weeks prior to the telethon in a high-traffic location, pleasing them even more. If you keep your promises, the donors will want to participate in next year's event. In a way, you are helping establish a format that hopefully can be adopted by next year's chairman. It will give them a plan, or at least a direction.

We need to keep reminding ourselves that the purpose of fundraising is to raise money, not to spend money. It is simple to write a check, but much more challenging to make proposals to underwrite the printing, talent, props, flowers, favors, wine, door prizes, transportation, hotel rooms, and limo services. You have to analyze each event to determine what your needs will be.

Public relations firms are available to represent charities for a fee, and there is nothing wrong in this. The out-of-pocket costs for the ad agency, as well as the purchase of time or space, can run into big money that most nonprofit charitable organizations don't have. But even when the work done by the public relations agencies is pro bono, the agencies get into the spirit of the competition. They go for the glamour causes. Professionals are sometimes reluctant to take on the lesser known causes. Everyone is willing to do commercials or ads for heart disease. The heart is beautiful and looks like a valentine.

It really is true, in the do-good industry, that sometimes you laugh to keep from crying. There are so many deserving charities and institutions, and so many activities that support them, the pressure is almost constant.

Commitment

You must believe totally in the cause you are championing, and in your own ability to carry out the plan and see that it is successful. Anytime you take on the chairperson's role, it becomes your plan, your brainchild. You have to stay with it no matter what obstacles you encounter. You must have the determination and *commitment* to see it through.

Your feelings about the work you are doing must be similar to the way that a musician feels his melody, an artist knows the canvas, a dancer moves. For example, if you are raising funds for the Leukemia Society, it is a good idea for you to visit the children in the hospital, see them in various stages of treatment, see what they have to do to live, talk with their family members. You will be motivated to do whatever it takes to help find a cure for this disease.

I try to know the cause well enough so that I can talk about it to others before I undertake the project. Therefore, people have confidence in what I am doing. This means I have to have a clear picture of what is needed. I make inquiries, ask questions, read the reports, visit the site, and understand the accounting. I have never been disillusioned, and, I hope, have never disappointed anyone.

In 1989 I made a commitment to serve as honorary chairman for the Houston Police Department's bicycle relay team, which raises funds for the Leukemia Society with a bike ride across thousands of miles. Twenty-four officers from the Houston Police Department would take on an ambitious 2,700-mile bicycle relay ride. What was unique about this is that they obtained their individual sponsorship through their own efforts, involving thousands of hours of personal time. I wrote hundreds of letters, sold T-shirts in shopping malls, and made myself available to assist the head of the relay team, Officer Al Skozen, in whatever capacity necessary. However, I drew the line at joining the officers in riding a bike to Vancouver, Canada.

A photograph was taken of the relay team and young leukemia patients at Texas Children's Hospital. We used the photograph for the front of a postcard mailing simply addressed to friends, and the choice was theirs to support the fundraising effort. A thank you for caring always makes the difference when you've had a positive response. Commemorative T-shirts and HPD caps were sold in area malls and at special events. In my letters, I hoped to secure several $5,000 sponsors. Some of the interesting incentive items we offered to sponsors were the commemorative team relay sponsor kits, engraved sponsor plaque, team photograph, and an interview and check presentation during the televent. We tried to encourage competition between the officers for sponsor funding. It added to the enthusiasm when several prizes were donated that could be awarded to the officers who raised the most funds. What makes this commitment so special is that the members of the relay team are so dedicated (and willing to get into excellent physical shape) to help those thousands of adults and children across the country who are battling leukemia for their lives. The total representing the yearly team effort is presented in the Leukemia Society's "Six Hours For Life" national telethon.

Detail

Over the years, I have developed what we jokingly refer to as a manifesto, a key to successful organizing. The manifesto gives a detailed written outline to every volunteer and donor/underwriter involved. It describes each person's responsibilities and gives a schedule of details. Every individual knows where the buck stops. In this way, everyone has a clear directive and, hopefully, nothing will slip through the cracks.

Later, as you move through these pages and on to the representative events I describe, you will see the microscopic attention to detail that is involved. One cannot do this work in a half-hearted way. The responsibilities are too important, the needs too great, and the competition too real.

You should expect the unexpected. When world-famous Spanish soprano Montseurat Caballe had to cancel her performance for the Society for the Performing Arts, there was double intrigue. This was the first event for the newly formed fundraising wing of the Society for the Performing Arts known as the SPA Angels. This group of participants pledged to make a minimum yearly contribution of $1,000. You simply cannot crater when your party, which is scheduled at a specific time, is suddenly moved forward two hours and you are short one honoree.

At the time of this event, I was married and my husband, Harold, liked to sing, so he took to the piano along with the general manager of the SPA, Leon "Pete" Petrus, who had a serious musical background. Pete delighted the guests with songs from "West Side Story" and "Tosca."

When you use male Runway Heart Throbs as fashion models, you will not have the following problem arise. However, with the "Women We Admire" fashion extravaganza benefiting neurofibromatosis, two of our honorees were pregnant. The event became more realistic and challenged the creativity of the Saks Fifth Avenue fashion coordinator, who produced the show. One aspect of the show was to allow each honoree to recognize the special man in her life. When one of the "Women We Admire" had two special men in her life and couldn't choose between them, I thought, why cause a dilemma for someone you are trying to honor? I simply said, "Have both of your special men." This happened with ABC's Channel 13 television anchor/reporter Melanie Lawson, who was torn between her father, the Reverend William Lawson, a respected member of our community, and her husband, Geary Broadnax, a professional photographer who would enhance any runway not only as a model but as a model husband.

When I was asked to chair the "Renaissance Evening" to benefit the Museum of Fine Arts in 1981, one of the main problems to consider was the fact that the museum had no kitchen. This made it difficult as we had planned to serve hot food at a seated dinner to all the patrons. We faced a similar problem in the Academic Court at

Lovett Hall on the Rice University campus for the Rice Design Alliance.

Don't be afraid to improvise. The challenge of working in an unusual setting produces wonderful results. I called upon Don Strange, a caterer from San Antonio who had gained prominence for his innovative catering during the Lyndon B. Johnson presidential era. Don had a reputation for handling any situation regardless of circumstances, including a no-kitchen factor. He prepared the food for both of these events, as well as the local Zoo Ball every other year. It was done with taste, no pun intended. Guests dined on avocado soup served in sculpted pumpernickel bowls, veal piccata, and other sumptuous delights served from thirty-two food service carts. Don's trademark carts reflecting our theme were decorated in pink, mauve, and gold.

With duplication of food items on the carts, we didn't have the problem of the long line syndrome synonymous with buffet meals. This alleviated people having to eat dinner at home before going to dinner.

As a special incentive to our $10,000 host tables at the Museum of Fine Arts for the first time, guests dined in the Weiss Gallery amidst the magnificent art. Uppermost in everyone's mind was the great care and consideration we had in regard to the art collection.

One detail you can't control nor always predict when hosting an event out of doors is the weather. I sometimes feel that I am blessed with a unique contract with God. I never have an alternative rain date, which sometimes makes my committee members break out in hives. Only once did I need to make a small concession when the weather was seemingly questionable for an outdoor affair. In anticipation of rain, we moved the tables under the arches in the Academic Court at Rice University's Lovett Hall. Just as the evening ended, the rains began to pour. Once more, we were dancing with fate and singing in the rain.

Decorations

You must take a step back in fundraising, close your eyes, and let your imagination flow freely. Repeating someone else's idea, or what has been done in the past, is not an exciting prospect. Decorating is costly, but with creative energy and resourcefulness, you can produce the ambiance you want.

At the Challenger Center benefit, the cost to decorate the grand foyer of the Wortham Center on the scale that was needed would have been astronomical. Instead, an atmosphere of patriotism was achieved with symbolic American flags, Sousa-style marches that filled the Wortham Center, an "Art in Space" exhibit from T. H. Rogers (a local school), space artifacts from the Museum of Natural Science, and a booth selling *Challenger* memorabilia, T-shirts, coffee mugs, and an MCA record, "The Mission Continues."

In 1988, for "A Step Back In Time," we enhanced the effect we wanted with appropriate and romantic favors donated by Neiman Marcus. For the ladies there were antique lace handkerchiefs, and for the men, bow ties. Ironically, the ties were such a hit that the men and women were fighting over them. The women had fun wearing the bow ties as headbands. Several months later, I ran into the head of a Houston law firm who was wearing a good-looking bow tie that I commented on. He said he was inspired by the bow tie he received at the Rice Design event and has worn one ever since. You can even become a trendsetter.

As the guests arrived, they were greeted by a quartet of chamber music from the Shepherd School of Music at Rice University. Arrangements of our native magnolia blossoms and jasmine-scented candles filled the air, and multi-colored banners attached to tall poles waved in the night. Table tops were laden with old lace, antique toys and candles, while the pink, gel-covered lights in the archway created a nostalgic journey back in time.

No seating arrangement should be considered routine or taken lightly. The seating may seem as basic as walking, especially if you sell an entire table. However, in less than booming economic times, even corporations and the affluent no longer buy entire tables. One of the pluses in purchasing an entire table was that you would know your dinner companions.

Tact is at a premium when arranging the seating. It is insensitive to seat a man's ex-wife at the same table as his current wife, or, in some cases, in the same room. To enhance the level of conversation at parties, it is a good idea to have smaller, more intimate gatherings. Assemble a diversified group of people who do not see each other constantly but who have similar interests and ideologies. You have to appeal to a mixture of people: some who like to dance, some who like to talk, and some who just enjoy being there. If you are trying to be witty and offer light remarks, remember only those tastefully delivered words can form the lasting memories of a party. In earlier times, protocol dictated that men and women separate after dinner and share those remarks that were for men and women only, respectively. You have to be careful, though, if you are one who is likely to be easily quoted.

People don't like to feel isolated. The atmosphere has to be upbeat, warm, and friendly. Whenever possible, thought should be given to seating people near those they know, would want to meet, or with whom they might share a bond. Seating your guests will bring out your diplomatic skills.

Media

No one engaged in fundraising should ever underestimate the importance of the media. Show appreciation whenever they have indicated an interest in your event and thank them sincerely for their support. Most nonprofit charitable organizations have an executive director, and I have found that press releases are best prepared in-house. Who knows better than the head of an organization about a disease, the needs of the organization, the research presently going on, as well as any significant progress and hopes for the future?

Your press releases need to be timely and cover all the important information. Anything that is newsworthy about the nonprofit organization, ranging from expanded hours, new personnel, features on the volunteers and recipients who have benefited from the programs, should be included. High-profile names attract attention. The press releases should be written on the letterhead of the organization.

Delegating

I have a tendency to try to do everything myself. This is neither good for me mentally or physically, nor for the morale of my committee heads. You must be able to delegate wisely and efficiently. Exercise great care, however, in choosing those to whom you delegate certain responsibilities.

If you discover that someone is not doing the job, you will have to work twice as hard to recover lost ground. Diplomacy is required here, and you will never be disappointed with a hands-on approach. Every detail has to be considered and each is equally important to the overall success of your event.

When organizing a committee, make certain the individual tasks are clearly defined. There should be someone who oversees these details to make certain they are being completed according to plan — a system of checks and balances. It is important to instill confidence in your volunteers. A clear understanding of tasks will help prevent under-utilized volunteers with better coordination and scheduling. Whenever volunteers answer a telephone at a nonprofit organization, they must be trained to give out correct and accurate information as well as be enthusiastic representatives.

Additional secretarial support may be needed during a campaign to handle correspondence and other tasks. Once you have given an event a specific date, it is a good idea to schedule the following year's event at the same time of the year. This gives your event continuity. If an idea such as the representational photograph for the "Evening of Hope" AIDS benefit becomes a successful logo, you can use it again, not only for the invitation cover, but for posters and public service messages in publications.

Always provide enough security to assure crowd control and the protection of valuable items that are part of a live or silent auction portion of the evening.

Recognition

Never forget that we all want to be appreciated for our efforts, and no one wants to be taken for granted. It is essential to bond with the people who make your event happen. You must be generous in passing out strokes, recognition, and thanks, which will in turn motivate volunteers even more to do a good job and insure their staying power as volunteers and supporters for your future fundraisers. Remember, thank-you notes are not just good manners, but good business.

At the *Challenger* post-gala celebration, the stars who donated their talent for the concert received honorary proclamations from former Houston mayor Kathy Whitmire and the city council. That was one way of demonstrating how much the community appreciated the performers' contribution of time, talent, and energy. The "Midnight with the Stars" supper and party at the Four Seasons Hotel afforded the *Challenger* families an opportunity to talk with the entertainers and guests on a more intimate level. I have a lovely letter from June Scobee telling me that I would always be a member of the *Challenger* crew family. Each family member was given three silver medals to present whenever and to whomever they chose. I received one that evening, and I shall treasure it always.

I complain about the demands, threaten to retire or take time off, but my enthusiasm for fundraising keeps growing and will always be in my soul. I must confess, I am hooked. It is my magnificent obsession. I sometimes feel like Addoo Annie in *Oklahoma*, who sang, "I'm just a gal who can't say no."

What I call having a ball is really my form of missionary work, improving the quality of life, addressing urgent community needs, honoring the worthy, and helping to maintain our arts and culture. I mentioned earlier that there are not many role models for those who volunteer to take up these causes. But several women have served as my personal heroines: Alice Brown, Carroll Masterson, Dominique de Menil, and Nina Cullinan, who have freely opened their hearts to the community.

Miss Cullinan was a classic example of that fine old phrase — a patron of the arts. She was an eccentric, no-nonsense straight-talker. This magnificent lady possessed a patrician air somewhat reminiscent of Jessica Tandy. Friends like to tell how Nina liked to be called Miss Cullinan rather than Miss Nina because the other sounded too "Old South."

I met her in 1979 when I was chairing the Houston Ballet Foundation Ball, "The Soiree on the Swanee." She came to my home for one of the pre-party functions, an afternoon party celebrating a young jewelry designer, Rebecca Collins from Dallas. The designer was happy for the opportunity to preview her designs among such distinguished guests, and she offered to donate a percentage of her sales to the ballet. This was one of those seeds that could have given life to the now successful Nutcracker Market that brings in needed revenue to the ballet. Rebecca Collins has a booth at the Nutcracker Market every year. New talents always welcome the occasion to broaden their base and meet new clients.

And so my friendship with Miss Cullinan began. Before she died, I had the privilege of honoring her in 1982 at an event benefiting the Archives of American Art, a respected national organization with its main offices in Washington and New York. Only because the cause was one she strongly believed in did Miss Cullinan, at eighty-four, agree to become the honored guest.

The Archives of American Art is a branch of the Smithsonian Institute founded in 1954 in Detroit by a group of patrons and scholars. Its role is to document the visual art history of the United States on microfilm. Today the Archives has more than eight million items available to thousands of qualified users. The Archives acquire material by donation or loan for microfilming. For example, you can find and read the life of Mary Cassatt, ponder the memorabilia of Thomas Hart Benton, study the sketchbooks of Elisabet Ney, or read the correspondence of Forest Bess. You can even share some of their private thoughts and darkest secrets.

This is one of those lesser known causes I've mentioned, but important historically as it documents the works, letters, memorabilia, and signatures of American artists. The Houston branch, begun in 1978, is located in the Museum of Fine Arts. It has amassed more than 440 collections across the state, documenting the art history of Texas. The pilot project was originally founded by the Brown and Kleberg foundations.

The theme of the evening centered around the preservation and appreciation of the cultural heritage of Texas. I felt it was important to focus on Miss Cullinan and her many contributions as a philanthropist to our city and state. She was a member of the Municipal Arts Commission, founding member of the Houston Ballet, and founding board member of the Contemporary Arts Museum. Prior to the founding of the Houston Ballet, Miss Cullinan would travel to see the Ballet Russe and other dance companies perform.

The funding generated by the tribute dinner honoring Miss Cullinan enabled the Texas project to complete another two years of work and created a solid foundation for future study on the visual arts of Texas. On the cover of the invitation was a collage by Dorothy Hood, an American artist who was documented by the Archives of American Art. The program for the evening gave the guests an idea of the schedule: cocktails at 7:30 P.M., with a listing of musicians, dinner at 8:30 P.M., remarks by the national director, William E.

Woolfenden, and the presentation of the proclamation by the mayor. A tribute to Miss Cullinan was written by the director of the Texas area project, Sandra Jensen. Miss Cullinan had given thousands of dollars to enhance the city, including the original $250,000 gift to build the Cullinan Hall at the Museum of Fine Arts. This was done in memory of her beloved parents.

By including a personal message in the program, people get a sense of why you are involved. It gives you the opportunity to acknowledge their support. This is especially true when an organization is not well-known and requires reaching out to build a base of supporters. Our event practically sold out after the invitations were mailed, and $250,000 was raised. Having an honoree like Miss Cullinan provided a big boost.

To add to the ceremony of the occasion, we used the Governor's Honor Guard from Texas A&M to form a saber arch for our distinguished guests to pass through. On display were photographs, letters and newspaper articles from the Texas Archives about Miss Cullinan and her gift of the Mies van der Rohe Cullinan Wing. As guests entered the hotel ballroom, they were surrounded by a mixture of music ranging from the Concerts Royaux to a trio called Montgomery, Mayes, and Stritch. (Today, the very talented Billy Stritch is performing with Liza Minnelli.) At this dignified event, the guests were dancing before dinner, during dinner, and after dinner to the Bob Hardwick Orchestra.

Former mayor Kathy Whitmire attended the event and issued a proclamation naming Nina Cullinan Day. Actor Jim Nabors flew in from Hawaii to be a part of the ceremonies, and opened the evening by singing the national anthem. Neiman Marcus CEO Philip Miller participated by providing the underwriting for the evening. The involvement of the for-profit sector as underwriters reflected their commitment in giving back and being a part of the cityscape. Famed fashion designer James Galanos, who was showing his collection at Neiman Marcus, rearranged his schedule so that he could attend the event. That evening, we introduced his fragrance, Galanos, and gave the perfume as favors.

In the end, the fragrance was the sweet smell of success.

CHAPTER 2

What's In It For Me?

Y ou might ask, why do I become involved? Everyone on this
wrinkled prune of a planet should want to make a difference, to
stand for something. You can do this by being the executive of a
company and providing leadership and guidance. You can be an
educator, a minister or a doctor — people who shape the mind and
mend the spirit and provide for the sick. These commitments are
part of the reason and meaning of life.

I feel strongly that community service is my calling. Maybe this is
my special art and talent in life. Who knows why? We are all given
different tasks. I know that this calling will always have a place in my
life. It has for more than twenty years. My work on behalf of others is
a cherished part of my life. I don't know if I subscribe to the theories
of astrology, but the description of an Aquarian suits me. According
to the astral charts, I am doing what I do best.

What is it that speaks to me? How do I determine which cause to
support? Those are tough questions. However, being a solitary human being does dictate some obvious limitations. Everyone has only
so much time, and that is why you should establish your own criteria.
"Why should I take this on?" you ask yourself. You have to balance
your life; the causes you undertake will be better served if you are
well-rounded. This becomes a form of personal juggling.

You may wonder, why chair an event to benefit the Houston

Ballet Foundation? For me it is the love of the artform and, in particular, dance. I admire the hard work and dedication of the artistic
director Ben Stevenson and how he has molded the Houston Ballet
into a company that ranks fourth in the nation. These fundraising
events are the means to an end. They fund world-class productions,
endow scholarships to talented and deserving students, and expand
the international nature and culture of a city. These are valid reasons
for one type of commitment.

With the "Million Dollar Evening," the benefit for the Stehlin
Foundation for Cancer Research, one didn't need to search for motivation. Everyone, through family or friends, has been touched by
this disease. We have progressed in the early detection and treatment of various forms of cancer. More research is critical if we are to
move forward to that final step: finding a cure for this destructive
and devastating disease. We have to nurture and encourage the Dr.
John Stehlins who look into the face of heartbreak and death on a
daily basis.

Consider the disease AIDS. It enveloped us like a plague. At
first, people wanted to wish it away. They wanted to sweep it under a
carpet. In 1987 my friend John Henry Faulk, the late folk humorist,
called me and said urgently, "We've got to help these people." He
had just come from a meeting at the Bering United Methodist
Church, and before boarding an airplane back to Austin called me
with tremendous concern.

At the time, he didn't realize he had cancer. John Henry had
planned to give a benefit performance of his one-man show for a
fundraiser. In his characterizations from "Deep in the Heart," there
was a father and mother who had not only just found out their son
was gay, but that he had AIDS.

So I took up this controversial cause. One of the goals that I
hoped to accomplish with this fundraiser was to emphasize the non-
controversial. I kept stressing the fact that AIDS was a community
health issue and not just a gay man's problem. To broaden the audience and base of support for this event, I also emphasized that the
funds would remain in Houston to help people here. The fundraiser
was linked to a church organization rather than a gay activist group,
and the focus was directed to patient dental care and compassion for
seriously ill people, including support groups and individual counseling.

Some "friends" stopped speaking to me briefly, but I had given my word to John Henry. They couldn't understand why I would get personally involved. This is when fundraisers have to be prepared to stand up for what they believe in. Even the more influential gay groups in the community didn't want to be involved, fearing the stigma associated with AIDS at that time.

People with AIDS were having difficulty in getting dental care because of fear, discrimination, lack of money, information, and insurance coverage. The dental society had been trying to open a clinic to treat people with AIDS for more than two years. They were finally welcomed with open arms by the Bering United Methodist Church.

This unique dental clinic was to be operated jointly by the Bering Church, and the Bering Community Service Foundation. More than twenty local dentists committed to donate their services on a rotating basis. With the "Evening of Hope," we were able to get an AIDS dental clinic up and running. Programs were established for support groups for families, women, and mothers, and more than sixty individuals began meeting weekly. A therapist and peer volunteers provided free counseling to patients with AIDS, their families, and primary caregivers. The daycare center provided supervision by staff and volunteers if primary caregivers were unavailable during the day. This was before AIDS became an "acceptable" and popular cause. The "Evening of Hope" broke down the barriers and united the city in support of AIDS research and care. The "Evening of Hope" fundraiser was the first fundraiser for AIDS in Houston to raise $100,000.

The Bering dental clinic is open to all HIV positive and indigent patients. Other funds raised provided emergency meals and medicine for AIDS patients and a support group at the Bering Church for female AIDS patients.

As a chairman of the Christmas Food Basket program for Volunteers of America, our goal was to provide a family with a basket of food for a Christmas Day dinner that would last several days. The Christmas Food Basket is one of the many services VOA offers to people in need. Throughout the year, VOA provides free clothing, meals for the elderly, and substance-abuse treatment programs for women alcoholics. VOA projects are supported entirely through donations. In Houston we served 2,000 families and 13,000 individuals in our first year – and that assistance grew by a third the next. With the economic difficulties Houston had been experiencing, the demand kept growing.

The funds I helped raise were spent to purchase items to fill the food baskets, such as eight to ten-pound hams, canned vegetables, dried beans, rice, bread, and powdered milk. Additional items, such as baby food, diapers, and toys, were provided if funds permitted.

Anyone undertaking a similar project needs to know who to contact. Helpful avenues I have found include meat packers' unions, large grocery chains like Randall's, local grocers' supply, wholesale food warehouses such as Sam's, and packing companies. Most of these businesses have charitable contributions in their budget and might be receptive to your proposal. A meat packers' union might make your group their specific volunteer project. Canned goods can be provided by a grocer's supply house.

You will read about the "Ham It Up" fundraiser I did in 1988 in the Pearls Before Swine chapter when I again served as the Christmas Food Basket chairperson. I enlisted the support of the owner of the Cadillac Bar in Houston, and they agreed to loan us their Party Shack for both events. They understood the benefit they would receive from the media coverage and the potential patrons who would attend. With some of our high-profile guests, the restaurant even began their wall of celebrity photographs. The first year's event was "Share Toys With Our Children For Christmas" party, benefiting the children involved in the VOA Christmas Food Basket program and the Star of Hope recovery centers. The Cadillac Bar provided their famous Cadillac buffet, mariachis, clowns, and a Harley Davidson biker who made a great Santa Claus. At this event we gathered over 300 toys, which were distributed equally to the children of both agencies.

I will never forget a letter I received signed by a "Mother in Need." She said she had been praying that "Operation Care and Share" would be able to help her give her son the only Christmas present he would receive, and somehow pay her rent as she had been unemployed. Not only did we try to make their Christmas happy, but we also referred them to an agency that would take care of their rent and utilities. Part of the VOA philosophy is for people to learn to help themselves and instill in them a sense of pride and a feeling of recovery. The joy VOA brings to the children in turn brings hope to their parents.

My first meeting with Tina Colaco, founder of the "Be An Angel" program at T. H. Rogers school, was a brown bag lunch with several of the teachers. They wondered initially if there were resources available in Houston that would fund enhanced communication devices and electric wheelchairs for the multi-handicapped students attending the school. I told them there were sources willing to lend support, and that it would probably work better to bring prospects to the campus. I took the public affairs director from the Ford Motor Company to the school. He was so impressed by what he saw that he proposed a matching grant of $15,000.

Once anyone entered this special and unique educational environment and felt the warmth and caring the teachers and volunteers exuded, they would be convinced and motivated to help. You have a real sense of what this school is all about and their great efforts to bring the handicapped students into society's mainstream. The lunches are prepared by handicapped students. It was the first school in the country to place programs for both the multi-handicapped and the gifted in the same environment. Funding for "Be An Angel" has been maintained through individuals, corporations, foundations, golf tournaments, and through the efforts of the Children's Fund and Charity Players.

In your city, there is probably an organization similar to the young Charity Players. This group is made up of young college graduate professionals between the ages of twenty-two and thirty-five. They put on fundraisers once a year and donate the proceeds to causes like the "Be An Angel" program. They investigate the cause on their own and determine their own criteria. One year they donated $30,000 to a playground project.

Bill Bradshaw is a landscape architect who designs adaptive playground space that is accessible to most any child. As with all the "Be An Angel" funds, these funds needed to be raised outside the school district. The cost of the playground project was $250,000, and the swimming pool, which provides therapy for the students as well as recreation, was already funded at $750,000. This meant total dedication and determination to make that dollar goal happen.

The "Be An Angel" golf tournament raised $60,000. In order to make any golf tournament work, your cause has to attract wide support. This requires sponsorship for each hole, goody bags, and underwriters if the tournament is to be profitable.

What came as an unexpected surprise to me was when Tina Colaco invited me to the school and asked that I bring several friends. The students gave me a "Carolyn Farb Day," which I shall always remember. In wanting to communicate with all the students, I asked one of the teachers to teach me to sign. Each of the groups, the gifted, the handicapped and the multi-handicapped, at the school participated. Should you find yourself in a similar situation, you should make the effort to communicate on a mutually acceptable level. I wanted to show my appreciation for the handmade Valentines and letters. That was a very special moment.

In my effort to bring people into the "Be An Angel" program at T. H. Rogers, I would talk about the school to friends in the media. Anchor/reporter Bob Boudreaux at Channel 13 was able to get coverage of one of the early golf tournaments. At that time, he was also a member of the Leadership Houston group and was so enthusiastic about the work Tina was doing for the children, he nominated her to membership. Within this group, she could meet other people in Houston to share ideas with and help the school.

All of this networking with people brings about immeasurable results. With the YWCA, I worked with someone at Panhandle Eastern and that same person did the invitations and printing for the San Jacinto Girl Scout Council. A presentation on fundraising which I gave before the Public Relations Society of America, Houston Chapter, brought me in contact with a great cross-section of people who make things happen in a city. I am always fascinated at how small the circle is and how productive it is to network with others.

Gloria Steinem is someone I have always admired for her efforts to help all women in their pursuit of human rights. You can imagine how flattered I was to receive a telephone call from her asking me to chair a benefit for the Ms. Foundation in Houston.

The event was called the "Stars of Texas Gala" and would take place in the summer. I knew this would be one of those events which would not be that easy. It was the first time that a major fundraiser had been held for the Ms. Foundation for Women outside of New York City. The success of this event would determine whether similar benefits would be feasible in other cities. The Ms. Foundation was not well-known or highly visible. The goal was to increase visibility so that other nonprofit women's groups would know to seek funds from the Foundation. Some of the key high-profile people on the host committee were Lieutenant Governor Bill and Diana Hobby, the mayor of San Antonio, Henry Cisneros, astronaut Sally Ride, and Senator Lloyd Bentsen.

The Stars of Texas Gala was to benefit the Ms. Foundation for Women, the first public women's fund that supports women and girls in need. The Ms. Foundation addresses basic survival issues in the area of women's safety, economic justice, and reproductive rights. Several of the programs that receive funding from the Foundation are centers for the prevention of child abuse, shelters for battered women and children, and job training and employment programs for women's groups.

A goal of $100,000 was set for this "Black Tie and Boots" Gala held in June of 1984. To establish a more secure base, I felt it was important to begin building a relationship with the corporate sector who provide employment to large numbers of women. Among the corporate sponsors were Houston Lighting and Power, Transco, and Security Control Systems. Volkswagen of America donated a new VW Scirocco for a door prize. Some of the stars who traveled to Houston were Ms. board members Marlo Thomas, Phil Donahue, Dabney Coleman, Marvin Hamlisch, and Loretta Swit.

People found it curious that actor Dabney Coleman, who is known for his roles of overt chauvinism in the TV series *Buffalo Bill* and in the movie *Nine To Five,* was one of our celebrity guests. Dabney remarked on the incongruity of what he does on television and in the movies and the causess he genuinely supports, such as the Ms. Foundation. As I am sometimes called a socialite, much to my chagrin, probably some people thought that I was perhaps out of my element. I like to use the term "humanist" instead of "feminist." Marlo Thomas felt there was money to be raised in Texas, women in need in Texas, and ideally, the gala would bring everyone together.

A treasure trove of great minds and wit assembled that evening, including such distinguished women as the state treasurer and later governor, Ann Richards, Sara Weddington, former aide to President Jimmy Carter, and Sissy Farenthold, once a candidate for governor. The key to the success of this event was attracting a group of supporters outside the circle that the public considered "feminist." We needed to reach the entire gamut of people. The crowd of 700 included a mix of politicians, feminists, and social types.

The event helped give a more accurate image of feminists. They can be glamorous, they are not all serious, they like to have fun, and they are people who just care about women's issues. Steinem commented, "This wouldn't have been possible ten years ago." I recall a favorite line in an interview I did with Gloria for *Interview* Magazine. Somehow we got on the subject of her liking to tap dance. I can see it now. She said, "I do it mostly in elevators when nobody is in there, just me and the Muzak. Then the doors open and there I am, arms akimbo, caught embarrassingly in mid-step. But sometimes when I am at home and just tired of sitting, I will get up and tap dance."

I had received a call from Lisa Turner, a freelance ABC reporter, who asked that I meet her and June Scobee for lunch. Right away I knew these tunafish lunches could get me into serious trouble. I had met June before and brainstormed briefly about the *Challenger* project. It seems Lisa had been advised to ask me to chair the Challenger Gala. All seven families of the *Challenger* crew were determined to turn their personal tragedy into a positive experience for our nation's youth, helping to prepare them for the technological demands of the future. It has always been one of my lifelong dreams to offer positive motivation to young people which can deter some of them from society's ills. The Challenger Center learning programs offer this. Not only are the Centers living memorials to the crew that perished, but they offer new and exciting learning opportunities in space science technology. Because I believe in the American dream, I had no choice but to accept.

They had been planning this event for months, and yet sixty days before the event, nothing had been secured. Channel 13 and Pace Concerts were involved, but there were no firm commitments. Our goal for the evening was to produce a concert that would be uplifting and patriotic in spirit, and we did.

After a series of phone calls and correspondence, I met with the president of the L'Alliance, the late Dr. Rameesh Adlakha; board member and honorary Belguim consul, Andre Crispin; and the school director of the L'Alliance, Claude Boutin. The Houston branch of the L'Alliance was like a best-kept secret. As it is with all nonprofit organizations, the L'Alliance was in need of funding. The group that gathered for the lunch meeting felt that if I would agree to take on this commitment, it would contribute to the strong relations between Houston and France.

The proceeds of the Bastille Day Celebration were ear-marked for the E. G. Leonardon Scholarship Fund at the L'Alliance Francaise. The Houston branch of the L'Alliance, founded in 1924, is the third largest with 500,000 members worldwide. The Leonardon fund was created in 1959 and gives scholarships to undergraduate students to study for a summer in France. This nonprofit organization brings together Francophiles of all nationalities to promote the language and culture. The students are given the opportunity to totally immerse themselves in the French way of life. In addition, each year a teacher is selected from the Houston Independent School District and receives a grant for a summer of study in France. Another objective of this program is to stimulate interest in international careers.

For the invitation design, we wanted to use an image that celebrated both Bastille Day and the bicentennial of the American constitution. We chose the state capital of Richmond, Virginia, designed by Thomas Jefferson from the Maison Carree at Nimes, France. Our Legion D'Honneur Medalist was Paul Charron, who at eighty-five had been likened to a walking encyclopedia. We included a paragraph in the text of the invitation honoring his contributions. There were also quotations on the American constitution from James Madison and from Alexis de Tocqueville. One of our board members, Pierre Escaron, who was with Schlumberger, took great delight in designing the invitation. It is important to encourage the involvement of your board. When there is a lot of copy, always look over text, as it is easy to miss an incorrect spelling of a word or simply a letter that was not proofread. As the design entailed a die cut, it became more complicated in the production phase, but was well worth the effort.

As a special highlight, a modern-day Will Rogers, the late John Henry Faulk, gave a special speech about the constitution. As a former recipient of the James Madison First Amendment Award, and someone who had been blacklisted during the infamous McCarthy era, this was very poignant. John Henry was an authority on the constitution. I had the privilege of introducing him.

The evening began with a cocktail reception and the opportunity for our guests to peruse the silent auction items. We chose a creative way to delineate the different levels of table supporters by making the table centerpiece or cloths slightly different. In the invitation, we distinguished our table sponsors by naming the tables Independence Hall, Constitution Avenue, and Place de la Bastille. Patrons could buy entire tables or individual tickets. Remember, always give those invited the opportunity, if they are unable to attend, to make a contribution to your cause. Our tickets were priced reasonably to generate interest in the L'Alliance Francaise. This is very important when you are first trying to take a growth step forward. Judged by how well you make your initial presentation, guests will want to attend the following year.

One of the cost-effective ways that we decorated the ballroom on a very limited budget was with the talent of balloon decorator Paula Weinstein, who created two connecting arches of balloons in patriotic colors that criss-crossed over the dance floor like the Eiffel Tower, festooned with ribbons.

In trying to create a special treat, I thought everyone might enjoy fresh baked goods the next morning. In talking with one of our board members who owned a well-known French bakery, I asked him if he would consider providing small panniers of croissants and brioches as party favors for our guests to take home. This hadn't been done before, and it worked well with our French theme and tradition. At the same time, our guests and supporters could reflect on the evening with their *"petit dejeuner."*

We did a tasting of the food and wines prior to the event. The salmon fume enticed the palate, and white wine was the overwhelming choice with the first course. When they brought in the Cherries Jubilee, the lights in the ballroom were dimmed and there was a flamboyant and dramatic presentation. In keeping with the charm of the French, the consul general of France presented me with a magnificent bouquet of flowers almost too big to carry.

It always fascinates me how people learn about other people. I call it unofficial networking. Sometimes it is word of mouth, destiny, osmosis, friends, or agency directors.

I received a phone call one day from Kent Waldrep, a young man who was injured while playing college football on artificial turf for Texas Christian University, in a game against Alabama. His spinal cord injuries motivated him to found the American Paralysis Association to bring people together who have suffered similar injuries. The American Paralysis Association raises funds for research.

Kent, who lives in Dallas, had asked me if I would work with him on chairing a film premiere in Houston. Prior to this, there had not been a fundraiser for spinal cord injuries in the city.

Kent had met actor Clint Eastwood, and Clint agreed that the American Paralysis Association would be the beneficiary of the world premiere of his next film, *Sudden Impact.* The evening would begin with a pre-party hosted in my home for the Gold Patron tickets, which were $1,000 a couple. Silver Patron tickets were $500 a couple, and they were hosted to a champagne reception in the Grand Ballroom of the Westin Oaks. The Gold and Silver sponsors would be united at the after-dinner buffet. The general screening tickets were $50 each. Knowing of Clint's fondness for Mexican cuisine, we served special miniature flautas and margaritas in his honor.

It was a case of Southern finesse and his commitment to the American Paralysis Association that persuaded Clint Eastwood to appear at the pre-function events. What was so incredible was his magnetism. Women followed him around, eagerly hoping to have a photo taken with him. As they were constantly closing in on him, I felt almost protective. Former mayor Kathryn J. Whitmire presented proclamations to Kent Waldrep, president of the American Paralysis Association, and to Clint Eastwood.

Everyone left for The Galleria in a caravan of limousines. Clint made an appearance at the champagne reception, walking through the crowd to meet the Silver sponsors before proceeding to the movie theater. Things settled down and everyone found their seat. I watched the movie from the back row of the theater with Clint and two of his friends. Being a brutal film with seventeen shootings, a rape, and the ultimate impalement of the bad guy on a carousel, there wasn't much to say as the film ended. To add a light note, being an animal lover, I commented that the dog stole the show.

The souvenir program is another way to raise money for an organization. For the Jack Benny Memorial Tennis Classic, which benefited the Juvenile Diabetes Foundation, my co-chairman and I raised $100,000. Actress Dina Merrill, a national board member of the Juvenile Diabetes Foundation, was instrumental in having Houston selected as the site for this annual tennis classic. Between the ads that were sold by our team members and the program sales, this was part of a successful formula for a number of years.

There was such an excitement in planning the celebration of the USO's 45th Anniversary Gala. The USO is dedicated to helping our American service men and women worldwide. By providing the comforts of home, a listening ear, and programs to help people adjust to military life, the USO serves as a constant reminder that those of us back home deeply appreciate the military's service to our country. The USO helps to soothe the problems caused by family separations, constant relocations, and unfamiliarity with foreign cultures.

This international gala took place on September 28, 1985, with who else but Bob Hope and other celebrities providing the entertainment, accompanied by the Glenn Miller and Tommy Dorsey orchestras. The event was held at the fabulous Dallas Loews Anatole Hotel. I was honored to have been asked to serve as the Texas gifts chairperson. This is another occasion to let your imagination roam. I tried to dream up unique items, to satisfy even the most discriminating patrons. You have nothing to lose by being adventurous.

I wrote to the office of the curator at the Department of State in Washington to see if a private tour of the diplomatic reception rooms could be arranged by that office. The tour would include a group of five people within a certain time frame. To make arrangements such as these, finding an introduction or suggestion of who you may write is helpful. Sometimes someone on the local or state level of government can give you direction.

English fashion designer Murray Arbeid, who made regular appearances at a local Houston department store, responded to our SOS by designing a lilac tulle ballgown and boa. When I was in Washington, working as state co-chair for the president's dinner, I had been invited on a cruise down the Potomac. I thought this would relate to the USO theme. I made a proposal to Commodore E. M. Skinner of the Presidential Yacht Charter, Inc., and he donated a cruise down the Potomac for twenty-four persons onboard the yacht *Independence*, with a stop at Mount Vernon for a tour. We managed to get a local caterer to underwrite the cruise. Former astronaut Walt Cunningham donated a priceless Apollo 7 flag from his personal collection of space memorabilia.

You can always go back to someone you have worked with in the past, if it turns out to have been a mutually pleasant situation for both. I wrote the managing director of Mottehedeh and they donated a glorious Hong bowl and stand. How about the world's most expensive perfume Pheromone, at $300 an ounce? Well, how would you like a one-pound bottle of Pheromone valued at $5,000? Helen Boehm donated a handsome pair of wooden ducks for the live auction. Judith Leiber donated one of her creations, an oval minaudiere starburst evening bag. Also donated for auction were a catered lunch for two and a balloon flight, a dinner party for twenty at the newest Hard Rock Cafe, a beautiful necklace from Bulgaria, and designer gowns from Mary McFadden and Bill Blass. Many of these items were placed in the silent auction, which took place from 6:00 to 10:00 P.M., and the live auction, which lasted from 7:30 until 8:30 in the evening.

When writing potential donors and making a specific request, I always give them a little history on the nonprofit organization, its purpose, and the people it serves. I try to explain the scope of the event and whether it is local, state, national, or international. If the monetary goal has been determined, that should be included in your presentation. Writing your correspondence on the organization's letterhead will give potential donors an idea of some of the people who are involved. They may recognize a name or know a board member. I try to provide as much detail as possible about the event, such as the general format for the fundraiser, the type of music and other entertainment. I also let contributors know how their donations will be acknowledged or listed in a catalogue and where items such as artwork will be displayed the night of the event. Depending on the size of their gift, and if the situation merits it, their tickets would be underwritten to the function.

In the case of the USO event, the donors were acknowledged in the *World Headquarters Newsletter,* which is distributed to 10,000 congressional and military officials as well as to 160 facilities worldwide. Appropriate literature on the organization providing additional information, press releases on past events, and a donor form should be enclosed. It is helpful if you ask for a response by a certain date. In this way, your request is not left open-ended and you can move forward if this doesn't materialize.

You have to realize that it takes time to build up your own reputation and track record, so don't be discouraged if you get a negative response. Just seek another avenue, another channel. If you keep accurate folders and samples of letters that you have written for past events, it will be helpful to you when you start a new project. You can also forward these personal archives on to the next chairperson.

In 1986 I was on a vacation in New Orleans and received a call from my friend Caroline Hunt. She had decided to include a commemorative program with the opening benefit for the Crescent. The

Crescent is a multifaceted shopping center, hotel, and office building complex that was designed by architect Philip Johnson. Her call came less than two months from the opening, and I could understand why she tracked me down. We didn't have much time, but I always work best under pressure. It gets my adrenalin flowing. This event would benefit TACA, a nonprofit organization, and would establish a million-dollar endowment for Texas performing artists at the John F. Kennedy Center for Performing Arts. (Just for your information, the initials "TACA" don't stand for anything.)

The gala ceremony was dubbed the "party of the decade." Celebrities from all over the country gathered for the three-day-long celebration. Robin Leach of *Lifestyles of the Rich and Famous* came with his camera. Among the guests were Perry and Nancy Lee Bass from Fort Worth; architect Philip Johnson; Jim Nabors; Roger Stevens, chairperson of the Kennedy Center; Ross and Margo Perot; London's Nigel Dempster; Governor Bill and Rita Clements, who chaired the gala; Helen Boehm; and Betsy Bloomingdale.

The event began with a cocktail party at the Crescent Art Gallery, followed by a black-tie dinner in the various shops and galleries of the complex. The food odyssey was prepared by thirty-five chefs, with food ranging from wild boar to pressed duck tamales. There was a tour the next day of the Dallas Museum of Art, followed by lunch at Bunker Hunt's Circle T Ranch. There you could view the Hunts' marvelous collection of Dorothy Douty birds and sense the Hunts' great family legend. Other homes included on the house tour through Highland Park were those of Governor and Mrs. Clements, Ed Cox, and the Trammel Crows. The gala culminated in the black-tie dinner held in the lobby of the Crescent Court. The table centerpieces were huge quartz and amethyst rocks ringed with white blossoms, greenery, and light from underneath that made them glow. This epic event truly reflected the lifestyles of the rich and famous and at the same time created a million-dollar endowment.

I accepted the program chairmanship because I felt it was important for the people of Texas to support the talented artists who live in Texas and provide for them to perform at Kennedy Center.

The full-page ads in the program sold for $5,000 each, the same price as the cost of the weekend for the Crescent Gala. I knew that an event of such grandeur might not occur again for a long time. The epic weekend would not only celebrate the establishment of the endowment but would provide a lasting memory for those attending.

In order to reach the goal of $100,000 for the program, I sent out 2,500 letters and averaged fifty telephone calls a day. In the letters I sent, it was important that the readers understand how their gifts would be used and why the endowment was so deserving of their support. The ongoing appeal of an endowment and widespread support is an attractive feature to someone making a decision to contribute. I tried to convey how they would feel about making this happen for the many talented performing artists in our state. There were forty full-page ads that brought in $100,000. It was a challenge to work between the two cities, Dallas and Houston, which are known for their competitiveness. As I was raising money for this nonprofit endowment, I used my zero-budget philosophy in negotiating the cost of paper, typesetting, printing, and photography for the program. I frequently had to fly to Dallas for meetings and to work on the program ad layout. Among those lovers of art and culture who rose above the two cities' competition were Dallas Museum of Art benefactor Wendy Reves and Houston philanthropist Jane Blaffer, who bought an ad for her Utopian community in New Harmony.

In June of 1985, Houston architects Irving Phillips and Peter H. Brown commissioned pianist/composer Paul English to compose a serious musical work that would serve as a musical tribute to the city of Houston and the state of Texas, each celebrating its 150th birthday in 1986. The concerto consisted of three movements: the first representing the future (electronics); the second, the past (chamber orchestra); and the third, the present (improvising quartet). The world premiere of "Neotexanaissance" was one of the first events officially sanctioned by the Houston Sesquicentennial Committee. Governor Mark White commissioned Paul, Irving, Peter, and myself as "Ambassadors of Goodwill."

Paul English would give two performances of his concerto in the Brown Auditorium at the Museum of Fine Arts. Although Paul was thirty-five at the time, he had already performed with great jazz legends Bud Shank, the late Arnett Cobb, Gladys Knight and the Pipps, and participated in jazz festivals worldwide. The concerto would also be presented as an official entry in the New Music America Festival of Houston. The concerto premiere was simulcast on public and classical radio stations. Tickets for the performance were $15 for the public and $12.50 for museum members, students, and senior citizens.

It was a unique musical project combining the elements of a traditional orchestra, contemporary popular idioms like jazz and country music, and computer-controlled synthesizers. The concerto painted an impressionistic view of the past, present, and future of Houston and Texas.

There were many considerations in working out the details with the Texas Chamber Orchestra, which would perform "Neotexanaissance" (New Texas Birth). As always, underwriting had to be obtained in order to give this gift to the city. We had to pay the orchestra members, print the programs, tickets, promotional material, and underwrite the reception following the concert.

A "Soiree Musical," hosted in my home, honored the special benefactors and prospective donors with excerpts of the concert performed by Paul English and musicians from the Texas Chamber Orchestra.

Whenever you are working for nonprofit organizations, you may encounter individuals who have their own separate agendas that are not harmonious with the expressed purpose of the project. Sometimes there develops a conflict of interest between the two different nonprofit groups that are trying to work together. Fortunately, the conflict that existed between the Texas Chamber Orchestra and the presenters never surfaced. It only gave minor anxiety attacks to those close to the issue. In fundraising, you have to be aware that these situations may occur and should be taken in good stride. It keeps you on your toes. Fortunately, with proposals that were made to the supporters of the Texas Chamber Orchestra, corporations, and philanthropic-minded individuals, the funding that was needed was accomplished.

I never have to wonder what I am going to do next. Opportunity not only knocks but rings my telephone. And, thanks to modern-day inventions, it sometimes arrives over the fax. I received a telephone call from the Menil Collection development director asking me if I would meet with one of my real life heroines, Dominique de Menil, the founder of the Menil Collection, and the director of the Menil, Paul Winkler. The Menil Collection was getting ready to open the "Robert Rauschenberg: The Early 1950s" exhibit on September 27, 1991.

"The Little Man" and "Tissue Paper" (Jakie Freedman and Carolyn Farb).

Carolyn Farb, Reggie Bibbs, and photographer Greg Gorman. My beloved grandfather, Jakie Freedman, instilled in me the idea of caring, of helping the less fortunate, of taking up a cause. The Texas Neurofibromatosis Foundation is one of those. Reggie Bibbs, an NF patient, serves as a great spokesperson.

The "Domain Privee," the Texas residence of Mr. and Mrs. Jake Freedman.

Chili's restaurant employees, NF poster representative Megan Phillips (on lap), executive director of the Texas Neurofibromatosis Foundation, Bob Hopkins. Your recognition and acknowledgment of volunteers will make them feel good about their contributions to your worthwhile organization.

NF volunteers Johnnie Howell, Darlen Cumby, and Ann Owens. A major phase of your fundraising event is to organize those angels known as volunteers.

A TRIBUTE TO

EXCELLENCE

"A Tribute to Excellence," benefiting the University of Houston's Athletic Department Scholar/Athlete programs, honored two of the world's greatest athletes, Olympic gold medalist Carl Lewis and Houston Rocket All-Star Hakeem Olajuwon, both ex-Cougars.

Carl Lewis, Carolyn Farb, Hakeem Olajuwon, and musician Ezra Charles. For the Gold underwriter tables at "A Tribute to Excellence," sponsors were invited to a special pre-reception with Carl Lewis and Hakeem Olajuwon and a photo opportunity with the honorees. (Courtesy Houston Chronicle)

The Challenger *tragedy left behind grieving families and a haunted nation. Our dream concert was an opportunity to channel those painful emotions into a positive, healing legacy. (*Moonwalk *by Andy Warhol)*

The Fabulous Thunderbirds lent a helping hand at the Challenger Center Concert.

The personal touch always makes the difference – it is often the deciding factor. Remember that competition is tight for the charity dollar, and as our economy fluctuates between highs and lows, it will become even tighter. (Photo by Eve Arnold)

As honorary chairperson for the Houston Police Department bicycle relay team, which raises funds for the Leukemia Society, I made myself available to assist in whatever capacity necessary. However, I drew the line at joining the officers in riding a bike from Houston to Vancouver, Canada.

Actor Jim Nabors flew in from Hawaii to be part of the "Archives of American Art" benefit and opened the evening ceremony with the national anthem. (Johnson Photography)

If one wants to be a fundraiser, one has to be flexible. There are not many role models in the field. You have to be able to trailblaze. (Photo by Manuel M. Chavez, courtesy Houston Post)

PROGRAM GUIDE

8
HOUSTON
PUBLIC
TELEVISION

Key Channel 8 volunteers and Astros TeleAuction Honorary Chairmen

Center: Carolyn Farb. Back row: Carol Ann Hamel, Kevin Bass, and Marilyn McCall. Front row: Jim Deshaies, Billy Hatcher, Lanier Wallden, Betty Little, and Alan Ashby.

In 1973 I realized, as chairperson of the Channel 8 Auction Super Sports Night, the importance of involving athletes in support of worthwhile causes. (Houston Public Television Program Guide, May 1988)

With KLOL Radio personality Dayna Steele. The media is an important ally.

Ken Waldrep of the American Paralysis Association, former Houston mayor Kathryn J. Whitmire, Carolyn Farb, and actor Clint Eastwood. A special appearance by Clint Eastwood at the pre-party before the world premiere of Sudden Impact *helped raise awareness and thousands of dollars for the American Paralysis Association.*

At the unveiling of "Passage Inacheve." In many ways, fundraising is as demanding as a full-time job, requiring a wide range of skills.

With cancer oncologist Dr. John Stehlin and my son, Jake Kenyon Shulman. Our goal for the Stehlin Foundation was to raise $1 million in a single evening to fund critical cancer research.

Art patron and philanthropist Dominique de Menil and artist Robert Rauschenberg at the Change, Inc. benefit, established by Rauschenberg to provide emergency assistance within a twenty-four-hour period to artists in need. (Annie Amante Photos)

Artist Robert Rauschenberg, Carolyn Farb, former Houston mayor Kathryn Whitmire. The Change, Inc. benefit celebrating the opening of Barney's New York and the Rauschenberg exhibit at the Menil Collection was one of those occasions where guests could not wait to get there and didn't want to leave. That is when you know you have scored a home run. (Annie Amante Photos)

The MAGAZINE

of The Houston Post

Nov. 8, 1987

How AIDS became a hot party ticket

Sometimes worthy causes can be controversial. The "Evening of Hope" benefit helped establish a much needed dental clinic for AIDS patients. Many groups, including the more established gay groups in the community, refused to become involved for fear they would be ostracized. They didn't want the stigma associated with AIDS at that time. (Houston Post, *November 8, 1987)*

Victoria Herberta, a homeless man who requested anonymity, Carolyn Farb, and Patrick Media executive Rob Schmerler. Jeffrey Jerome, a celebrated hog, became the official mascot for the homeless. The fight to keep Jeffrey Jerome's home within Houston city limits became international in its scope.

With humorist John Henry Faulk. John Henry and I talked about the upcoming "Evening of Hope" fundraiser that would help raise money for a dental clinic for patients with AIDS, emergency meals, medicine and support groups.

Ben DeSoto / Chronicle

Gloria Steinem, left, joins Carolyn Farb, who chaired the honorary host committee for the Ms. Foundation's Stars of Texas Gala.

Steinem, Farb join in making feminist gala successful

The Stars of Texas Gala benefited the Ms. Foundation for women. (Photo by Ben DeSoto, Houston Chronicle)

Former Houston mayor Louie Welch was the subject of intense media interest at the "Evening of Hope" after his much publicized "shoot the queers" remark. Our event gave Mayor Welch the opportunity to make amends.

Neiman Marcus general manager Gayle Dvorak, NF Board President Andy Gueverra, Carolyn Farb. You must believe totally in the cause you are championing and in your own ability to carry out the plans.

Neiman Marcus general manager Gayle Dvorak, Megan Phillips, Carolyn Farb. February 14, 1991, was officially proclaimed "Megan Phillips Day" by Houston Mayor Kathryn J. Whitmire during the "My Heart Belongs To Daddy" festivities. Megan was our neurofibromatosis poster child for the event.

Being an artist who is simpatico with fellow artists, Bob founded Change, Inc., a nonprofit tax-exempt foundation, in 1970. Change, Inc., assists artists of all disciplines in need of emergency aid. Grants cover rent to avoid eviction, medical expenses and unpaid utility bills, fire damage, and any other situations deemed by the Board of Directors as an emergency. It was his wish to combine his opening at the Menil with a benefit for Change, Inc. I was asked to chair this in conjunction with Barney's New York, who had underwritten the catalogue for Bob's show. They were opening their new store at The Galleria at the same time. Art being one of my great passions in life, I simply couldn't resist the combination of Dominique, Rauschenberg, and the cause.

When we first began talking, we had to figure out how to move guests from one venue to the next as effortlessly for them as possible. Sometimes you have to throw ideas out to determine what is and what isn't feasible. When there are several groups involved, you have to realize that each has its own agenda, but you have to look at the big picture. Barney's New York wanted to show off their new store to Houston and support a worthwhile organization at the same time. Everyone had heard about the celebrities that shop at Barney's, including Madonna and Warren Beatty.

The Menil Collection was happy to have Change, Inc., be the beneficiary, and I as the chairman would have the responsibility of creating an event that would both interest people in the cause and entertain patrons as well. Change, Inc., is not a well-known organization, so I immediately had to get information out to the media to raise the level of public awareness.

The foundation helps artists all over the United States, so I set out to find which ones in Houston had received assistance. Jesse Lott, a folk artist, had recently received a grant to help him with expenses after his studio had burned. A story was written about him in the *Houston Post,* and that qualified as his proposal to the foundation. We appeared together on a local television show, *Good Morning, Houston* with Lisa Trapani and Don Nelson, in order to inform potential supporters that the foundation was valid and did help artists in need almost within twenty-four hours. Jesse talked about the funds he received from Change, Inc., and several pieces of his work were on view. I talked about what a fun event the benefit would be and how people could purchase tickets. I pointed out how generous artists are to innumerable causes when they are asked to donate works of art. And I added that since some receive few monetary benefits and have hard struggles most of their lives, this fund was a lifesaver in emergency situations.

In the beginning planning sessions, it was thought some of the patrons who bought more expensive tickets would be hosted to a dinner in the private galleries of the Menil. I decided to make the evening less complicated and have one ticket price of $125 per person. To make certain that many of the artists would be able to attend, a minimum of $35 per person was charged, and for those who could not afford the tickets, underwriting was obtained.

Guests would go first to Barney's for the cocktail reception and enjoy its New York-style entertainment and food. Following that, they would attend the Rauschenberg exhibit and dine on Cajun cuisine and dance to the sound of a Cajun band, Beausoleil. There was a lot of telephone work and on-site meetings with Barney's in designing the invitation and planning the event. The handsome, onion-skin invitations tucked into miniature Barney's black shopping bags made quite an impression when they were received in the mail.

The 600 guests who attended, a mixture of the art, social and sports worlds, really added to the high energy and excitement everyone felt. The presence of Warren Moon and Ray Childress of the Houston Oilers, along with Olympic Gold Medalist Carl Lewis, had other guests standing around literally celebrity gawking. Walter Hopps, who curated the Rauschenberg exhibit both in Washington and at the Menil, was reminded of when he lived in Los Angeles, where the key to any event is in the mix.

The benefit raised public awareness about the foundation and was a great success. It was one of those occasions when people cannot wait to get there and don't want to leave. That is when you know you have scored a home run.

I like opening my home to others, whether it is to a group of bright children from the Wilhelm Schole, who enjoy looking at art and singing carols, or to myriad performing arts groups and medical causes, like the March of Dimes, Harris County Medical Auxiliary, or Holly Hall Retirement Center.

When I was asked to serve as honorary chairman for Project Coffee, which would launch the Harris County Medical Society's auxiliary community health project, I wanted to do a grown-up show and tell, so that the members would know exactly what their obligations and responsibilities were. We arranged to have the giant, circus-colored van named Health Adventure park outside my home. You couldn't miss the vehicle, and it definitely caught the attention of those who drove past. Guests could climb on board the forty-six-foot trailer containing the health exhibits and displays that the elementary schoolchildren would be seeing, and they could have a similar learning experience as the young children about health.

Members of the auxiliary were given the opportunity to volunteer for the two- to three-hour shifts and familiarize themselves with such community projects as the infant car seat loaner programs and alcohol- and substance-abuse centers. In several rooms of my home, we had lectures and demonstrations going on. Even as early as 1984, these members were already aware and involved in projects across the nation aimed at educating the public about child abuse.

Miraculously, with the diversity of causes and the thousands of visitors who have passed through my home, we have never had any losses. Indeed, someone special watches over us.

When I am caught up in the excitement of an approaching event, I sometimes can't sleep. I find myself unable to turn off the ideas and the details that play on my mind. I would like to start making my first phone calls at 5:00 in the morning, although this might not be the hour of choice for the person on the other end of the line.

What makes the efforts fulfilling are the many gestures and special moments, and the feeling of knowing you made a difference. Bringing the first Challenger Learning Center to reality was an indescribable experience. I got goosebumps knowing that my telethon for United Cerebral Palsy raised $650,000 in 1990 and passed the $1 million mark two years later. Goosebumps are an important barometer for me.

Nor will I ever forget receiving a poem about angels, dedicated to me, with an accompanying scrapbook of letters from gifted and handicapped children. They were students at T. H. Rogers school, a jewel in the crown of the Houston Independent School District, showing a bond can work between the students and teachers. It also works for people like me, who are privileged to play a brief part in such a rewarding experience.

The reward for hard work is walking into the ballroom at the Warwick Hotel and being the only individual alongside huge corporations to be honored by the Challenger Center, and having a school principal reach out to touch you as you walk by. It is that brief, special time when the band strikes up or the audience gives you a standing ovation for the "Evening of Hope" at the Alley Theater, and you know deep inside that your efforts succeeded. To think that we raised $100,000 for programs at the Bering Community Service Foundation when they had originally hoped to fill a church basement and raise $10,000. My advice to them was to think big. I hoped that I gave the AIDS issue the acceptance that it needed to go forward at that time.

It is seeing with your own eyes the joy, relief, or hope you have given to others, the kind of connection that makes your life have meaning. It is hearing from the children you encouraged in the pursuit of their dreams to become doctors, scientists, astronauts, or artists. It is all the people whose lives will be better, people whom you may never have met. It's humanity.

This is not meant to invoke pathos. These are my beliefs — that part of my role is to be a catalyst to transport the energy of others to the right destination. If some of this sounds mystical, that's all right. Some of it is. There is a thrill, a satisfaction, in realizing these sweeping goals that we hope will help the just cause.

It is the feeling of surging forward, of not accepting the initial negative responses. It is the small victory when another door opens and knowing your efforts may make it easier for the next Sally Ride to fly to the moon, or at least to have been given the choice.

Passion is a major ingredient of what I do — immersing myself totally in a project, determining the standards to be met and the ethics involved, harnessing ways to accomplish them, and always testing.

What's in it for me? All of the above.

CHAPTER 3

Creative Concepts

You have to be motivated in order to be creative. How do you capture that sense of commitment? First, you have to bond with a needy and worthwhile cause, something you truly believe in. You must want to make a difference in an individual's life or to better a community situation.

It can be helping with the expense of a specially equipped wheel-chair for a multi-handicapped child. A community need could be answered in the founding of an AIDS dental clinic, raising funds for cancer research, filling Christmas food baskets for a needy family, or founding a clinic to combat an uncommon disease. When something touches you, then you will find the creativity and the inspiration from within for a concept and the appropriate fundraising vehicle.

The concept may take shape in various forms, such as a roast, ball, gala concert or evening. It can be a fundraising luncheon format with a fashion presentation or a distinguished guest speaker. A tele-thon works well for medical causes such as United Cerebral Palsy, especially when children are the benefactors. Today there are many fundraising formats, such as walk-a-thons, theater benefits, celebrity waiters and waitressing, comedy relief and rock concerts, all working toward a common goal.

The next step after being motivated is to develop the creative concept. Your creativity will set your event apart from the multitude of others and make your cause a success.

If the vehicle is a gala evening, a theme adds another dimension. In planning publicity, campaign strategy should have continuity. With "I've Got A Crush On You," the second annual benefit for neurofibromatosis, the nostalgic appeal of the song was effective in initially getting the attention of the public.

Our theme honored "Women We Admire" on the eve of the traditional celebration of Mother's Day. We also recognized that special man, be it a father, husband, son, mentor or teacher, in the life of women we admire. Throughout the campaign our logo — the man holding a bouquet — would reinforce our theme of values, romance, caring, and nostalgia.

We raised funds for neurofibromatosis by appealing to both the heart and the mind. This is the opportunity for you to have fun and be creative. Be careful not to repeat an idea that has been done in the past. Try to be original. You must realize that when you do develop a fresh concept, it will become public domain and used in a diluted form by others. The ego has to let it go.

At the "Tribute to Excellence" benefit, the University of Houston scholar athlete program, it was natural and effective to have the Cougar Dolls perform a special cheer for our honorees on the steps of the River Oaks Country Club. They had worked out a routine for our honored athletes, Carl Lewis and Hakeem Olajuwon. In trying to achieve an effect suitable to the occasion, with a very limited budget, I convinced the athletic director, Rudy Davalos, to let us use their hard-won trophies as table centerpieces. These trophies had never left the campus. The coveted honors highlighted the past accomplishments and history of the school's teams and its athletes.

You can choose a theme that will complement your organization. For the Museum of Fine Arts benefit, I chose a "Renaissance Evening." This theme lent itself to many creative possibilities since one of the prize paintings in the museum's collection was from that period. We used renaissance images from their collection, not only for the invitation cover and poster but for all the printed material relating to the event.

When attending the first Reagan-Bush inauguration, I was inspired by a commemorative plate given as a favor to the guests at a candlelight dinner at Kennedy Center. I noticed on the back that the plates had been commissioned by Mottehedeh. In my efforts to explore and create new ideas for fundraising, I commissioned the potter Mottehedeh to make a commemorative plate of Bayou Bend. I wanted to do something other than door prize tickets, and this idea would focus on the museum's great American Collection at Bayou Bend, a gift from Miss Ima Hogg.

The Bayou Bend drawing that we selected was by the late artist Buck Schiwetz. In 1954, Buck had visited Miss Ima Hogg at Bayou Bend. They enjoyed a fried chicken picnic lunch together on the grounds, and later that same day he did the sketch. The handsome plates, a limited edition of 7,500, commemorated the date the museum began in 1924 and sold for $35 each.

Mrs. Mottehedeh flew to Houston through a terrible thunderstorm, but she was so enthusiastic about the commission that the storm didn't upset her. The plates were done in sepia on off-white porcelain and could be purchased singly or in sets. At the time, David Warren was the associate director of the Museum of Fine Arts and the curator of Bayou Bend. He oversaw the print transfer in Florence, Italy. The plates were finished in a kiln in Portugal.

How to package the plates was an important consideration. A taupe-colored box was our final choice, with the Mies van der Rohe logo on the front. I drafted a letter to museum members and enclosed an order form for the plates, should they wish to make advance purchases. This was a way for them to support the museum and have a lasting remembrance of Bayou Bend.

You set the tone for your theme with the pre-event invitation and any press you might be able to garnish for your cause. It is a building process, so that there will be constant momentum leading up to the actual event. For example, costumer Terrie Frankel was on a plane and read Madeline McDermott Hamm's story in the *Houston Chronicle* about the "Renaissance Evening." This spurred Terrie to write to me about how her costumes would reflect this richly historical period and might inspire guests to frolic and flirt while donned in royal attire during this glamorous evening.

In order to carry out your concept, you must be able to put your theme in motion. With my zero-budget philosophy uppermost in my mind, I had to try to think of ways to recreate this elaborate renaissance period. Luckily for me and quite coincidentally, the Texas Renaissance Festival, which is held annually in nearby Magnolia, Texas, was scheduled to begin in the same time frame. I went there to see if they would consider participating in our event. In a way, I explained, it would serve to let people know that the Texas Renaissance Festival was opening and would create a marvelous backdrop for our theme.

The festival was a treasure trove of exactly what I envisioned: Merlin the Magician, jugglers, fire eaters, face painters, dueling swordsmen, French and Spanish courts, magicians, tarot readers, palmists, gypsies, and belly dancers. The festival organizers liked the idea and agreed to participate in the evening. This helped complete our concept so that as the guests arrived, they were greeted by various talent in the form of music and people dressed in authentic costumes.

Our theme and concept were enhanced by the costumes the food service people wore. The thirty-two food service carts were festooned as well. The classical facade of the museum looked dazzling with pink lights and colorful banners. Red-vested car parkers greeted guests, who were then royally welcomed by King Henry VIII.

People-watching is always an important part of a gala evening. Among the guests at this event were French sculptor Miroslave Brozek, Brigitte Bardot's roommate for years; Count and Countess Alfred de Marigny, whose autobiography, *A Conspiracy of Crowns*, has been recently published; and even the late Judge Roy Hofheinz, builder of the Astrodome, who came in his wheelchair. The memories still linger of musical groups playing the recorder, oboe, and viola, neatly tucked away in the niches throughout the museum. One could marvel at the sword swallowers on the steps of the museum, and in the distance watch the dueling swordsmen in the sculpture garden or enjoy the belly dancers enticing guests in Cullinan Hall.

Using the original entrance to the museum added to the sense of history. The choice to have the event inside the building was innovational. The $10,000 hosts dined in the Weiss and Jones Galleries on tables covered in gold lamé. Each centerpiece was a work of art, a still life with a cornucopia of pomegranates, melons, and other fresh fruit spilling onto the tables in a grand manner.

Part of my zero-budget planning is to reach as many potential underwriters and benefactors as possible. Every dollar amount of underwriting you can realize translates into a dollar more that you are raising for your nonprofit organization. We were able to get the $1,500 worth of fresh fruit donated for the centerpieces from the grocery family, Jim Jamail and Sons. Twelve hundred guests from all over the world attended the ball. On the state level, officials included Attorney General Mark White and his wife Linda Gayle, and State Treasurer George Strake. From the ballet world came famed Russe prima ballerina Maria Tallchief and her husband, Henry Paschen, Jr.

A record-breaking $480,000 was raised. Today there are many activities that take place in museums all over the country, including very social weddings, corporate functions, upscale singles mixers to promote a membership drive, film screenings, auctions, and lectures. Museums are places that truly live and breathe.

Whenever I take on a fundraising assignment, there is a new excitement about what the plan will be. How will I be able to raise the funds and have supporters happy about being there?

Remember when we were all children (some of us probably still enjoy thinking of ourselves in that way) and we would daydream and imagine different fantasies? We traveled in our minds to far and exotic places, ruled imaginary kingdoms, became the princess being rescued in the tower or visited Africa by flying through the air like a performing member of the Wallenda family. I could go on and on. This is what you have to do. Don't set boundaries on your imagination to come up with a dream for your fundraising effort.

Once you establish the concept, you must then make it work.

If it is a telethon, be creative and think of a unique location. Where will this be held? What will take my event out of the realm of ordinary? I had my heart set on the covered skating rink at The Galleria Shopping Mall for the United Cerebral Palsy Starathon '90. I must confess, I could have made an easier choice.

The availability of the skating rink was the first consideration. A proposal was made to the decision makers at The Galleria, and they agreed to close the skating rink and give us the two days we would need to set up. We then had to find someone to underwrite feeding our 700 volunteers. Chili's, Inc., adjacent to the rink, was the perfect choice to cater our event if they would agree. Their menu was a perfect match as well.

A telethon depends upon a tremendous number of volunteers. Usually the volunteers prefer to have their refreshments before their shift begins and sometimes afterwards. When they arrive, they need to know where to meet. We had an on-site orientation, and then volunteers went out onto the rink, which no longer looked like a skating rink. It looked like a television studio.

Before I took on the chairmanship of the Starathon '90, I wasn't aware that practically all the money is actually raised before the telethon ever goes on the air. Most of the funds are pledged and committed well in advance. It is like having insurance. Whatever you raise on the air is a plus.

Once these two major essentials of location and catering were established, I could move on to the next in a series of steps to implement the dream. A manual was part of what came with the request that I take on the chairmanship. I must confess I never opened the book. I'm certain this tested the nerves and confidence of the telethon coordinator, Manny Mones.

I wanted to do something unique with our telethon to help children with cerebral palsy. Houston is a leader in the excellent care UCP gives to patients and their families.

The movie *My Left Foot* helped many to realize that people with cerebral palsy are not retarded. They want to be given the opportunity to live as normally as possible in our society. The movie focused on the brilliant Christy Brown, a young man who learned to communicate with his left foot. I purposely saw that movie shortly before the telethon was scheduled to begin, and I cannot tell you how touched and motivated I was.

The United Cerebral Palsy Center also works with children who have developmental disorders. The condition is caused by damage to the brain during pregnancy or birth, and, in some cases, through child abuse. A management program starts with attention to the child's movement, learning, speech, hearing, social and emotional development. The programs at the Center include therapists, educators, social workers, and other professionals who assist the family as well as the child. Certain medicines, surgery, and braces are sometimes used to improve nerve and muscle coordination. Our United Cerebral Palsy has the largest infant program in the state and offers it at no cost.

Starathon '90 came in second in the nation, raising $650,000 — and it was only our third year. I am proud to say that in 1992, they raised over $1 million.

Some of the luxury items featured in this telethon auction were a trip to Vienna, donated by the Austrian National Tourist Office (six nights in Vienna and six nights in Salzburg, transportation provided by American Airlines, hotel accommodations compliments of the

Hyatt Regency), and a James Galanos burnt orange, brown, and green print chiffon dress valued at $7,390.

Even though there may be hard and fast rules already established for a telethon before you take on the challenge, don't let that limit your creativity. And never hesitate to initiate a new idea or change an old one. You may decide to hold the auction of luxury items at a separate event. In this way, you would have a definite dollar figure beforehand. As I mentioned, most of the funds are committed in advance of the telethon airing. The auction now is held at Tony's Restaurant, where high-price bidders make a strong financial commitment to the telethon in advance.

You can continually redefine a fundraising concept. The UCP kickoff party in October launched our campaign and our goal. A crowd of 200 gathered at Jack's Restaurant, where the chef conjured up a southwestern menu complemented by coyote cocktails. Brandy Brown, former child lead in *Les Miserables* on Broadway, added her special talent to the evening. Brandy had participated in the Challenger Gala. Carl Lewis, the Olympic gold medalist, was on hand and, much to everyone's delight, sang a couple of songs.

Corporate and VIP sponsors were recognized at the pre-telethon party. The VIP sponsors were a new idea that I created for volunteers. In order to qualify as a VIP, the volunteer had to raise a minimum of $1,000 prior to the telethon. The VIPs had the choice of making this contribution personally or raising the money from several contributors. VIP incentives included such perks as sitting on a special VIP phone panel during the telethon, with an introduction on the air by one of the television hosts, and being invited to all the pre-events, like Sportsmania, the VIP Kickoff, and victory parties.

Corporate sponsors would be recognized in several different ways, including a direct advertising investment, a promotional event, and an in-kind donation of products and services. There were Bronze, Silver, and Gold Star packages that started at $500 and ranged upward to $10,000. Included in the Bronze package were the following: the corporate sponsor would be recognized during one local segment of the telethon, have one seat on the phone panel, and be given a one-minute live interview.

At the pre-party called Sportsmania, the live auction included priceless gifts such as a Ranger baseball with Nolan Ryan's signature, a golf game for two with Channel 13 commentator Marvin Zindler (including breakfast and lunch), a free-throw shooting contest before or after a Houston Rockets practice with Hakeem Olajuwon (including signed shoes, jersey and jacket), and an Astro Fantasy Camp for a father and son provided by the Houston Astros. President and First Lady Health and Racquetball Clubs donated two one-year memberships, and Mary Lou Retton donated a gymnastic lesson at Bela Karoli's gym (including lunch and autographed Pony tennis shoes).

Other priceless auction items were a signed Hank Aaron ball from the personal collection of former Astros player Norm Miller (now the Astros' marketing director), a dinner for eight with Hakeem Olajuwon at Carrabbas, a chance to "Go For The Gold" by running a sprint with Carl Lewis (including signed track shoes, T-shirts, and other sports items from the Santa Monica track team), a dinner for ten cooked and served at your home by former Oiler quarterback Dan Pastorini, an invitation for a father and son or daughter to attend an Oiler practice (as well as receive an autographed ball and personally meet Warren Moon and Ray Childress), tickets to the Pro Bowl in Hawaii (with air transportation provided by American Airlines and hotel accommodations by the Hyatt Regency Waikiki), a lesson in how to play quarterback by Warren Moon (with a signed official game jersey and autographed *Sports Illustrated* poster) and four tickets to the last game of the season.

Well-known auctioneer Jerry Hart agreed to handle the auctioneering chores. The event took place in what was then unfinished space on the top floor of The Pavilion.

During the evening, several of the sports celebrities, including Warren Moon and Ray Childress, were so caught up in the spirit of the evening that they even added to their already committed auction items. Mary Lou Retton personally auctioned off her gymnastic lesson. Putting the fun in your event makes the difference.

Our goal for Sportsmania was $50,000. The price of admission was a minimum $25 contribution to UCP. Three hundred guests attended and enjoyed rubbing elbows with top Houston sports celebrities. The Pavilion restaurants provided a diverse and exotic menu for the event. Some of the food delectables ranged from Hunan's famous orange beef, and Sfuzzi's baked eggplant and tomato torta to Cafe Express' spicy chicken salad and heavenly brownies. Atwood and Comeaux wowed the audience with their Broadway voices. Libations were donated by Miller Brewing, a national corporate sponsor of UCP, and Quality Beverage.

Remember, I have stressed how important it is to reach out and pursue all avenues of making contact with the public. The top money-maker that evening was the trip for four to Hawaii for the Pro Bowl. The high bidder was a lady who had caught a forty-five-second interview that I did on Channel 11's "Quarterback Corner" with Warren Moon and Gifford Nielson. She decided to attend the event at the last moment and won the trip with the top bid of $3,200.

On the evening of Sportsmania, a jeweler in the same center was hosting its annual holiday party, which meant our valet parkers had to be located at one entrance and theirs at another. It was an interesting interplay, as they would have loved to have our sports celebrities attend their event, since they generate so much excitement, and we would have liked some of their high-rollers at ours.

Keeping our music from drowning out one another was a challenge as well. When selecting a date, remember to check the local calendar of special events in your city, or an invitation service when available. Even in doing this, there are so many activities going on that it is almost impossible to select a clear date. Weekdays provide the better opportunity. It's your decision as to the day you select, a toss of the coin. The end of the week (Wednesday through Friday) finds people who work more willing to accept invitations. However, off nights (Mondays or Tuesdays) lend themselves to negotiations with restaurants, hotels, talent, and other potential underwriters.

When you are organizing a live auction, it is a good idea to limit the number of items to minimize the interruption of people having a good time. Have your star items included in the live portion and tailor your auction items to your audience. When you can, involve an experienced auctioneer. This will provide assurance that you reap the maximum funds from your donated items. With priceless items such as the signed Hank Aaron baseball, the amount of money you can raise is wide open, depending on who is in your audience. Be sure that the chairperson or auctioneer lets the audience know several times during the evening when the live auction will begin. If someone is raising a hand to respond to an auctioneer, provide an adequate number of volunteer spotters in the audience to recognize these individuals. The volunteer will then hand the information on the high bidder to a runner, who will take it to the volunteer at the recording desk. Next to the stage at the Sportsmania event, a UCP volunteer recorded the successful bid and was responsible for handling the financial transactions when the auction concluded. Sometimes you will have two people bidding on the same item. In a case like this, the decision rests with the auctioneer.

All of the donated items were either dropped off at the UCP offices, if that was convenient for the donor, or picked up by a crew of volunteers. In the silent auction, there were so many different gift certificates, memberships, restaurant dinners, sports shopping sprees, signed memorabilia, golf bags, and sports clothing that our guests received good value with their bids and contributions. All of these items were carefully displayed with a clipboard, pen, and bid sheet beside them.

As guests arrived, they could look over the items in the silent auction and go back throughout the evening to place a bid. Starathon '90 volunteers served as security to make certain that the items were picked up by the correct winning bidder. They also watched their tables during the evening to make sure that the proper clipboard was in front of the correct items and that everything was neatly arranged.

How you present your idea and carry it forward has to reflect your personal flair. You should regard every detail as paramount, and this will influence all your presentations.

In making the presentation to Hyundai America for the dream item of the telethon auction, UCP agreed to provide five slots on the phone panel during any two shift periods selected by UCP, and a couple of two-minute live interviews during the telethon related to the auction of the car.

The television station agreed to script and schedule the shooting of a one-minute corporate commercial. A Hyundai logo was imprinted on 2,000 posters that were displayed throughout the city. Their logo flanked the tote board during the telecast, and the donated car was displayed at the VIP corporate sponsor kickoff, at the December Sportsmania auction at The Pavilion, and on The Galleria Level One three weeks prior to the telethon. The car was even presented at a function the association of car dealers was hosting.

We presented the car with the minimum bid featured on a placard revolving on a platform packaged with bows. We were fortunate to get a car donated without strings.

Remember to use creativity in the planning of any type of event. If you commentate a fashion show, a refreshing approach is not to feature the clothes but to focus on the individuals who are modeling.

This will soften the commercial aspect of what you are doing, and the clothes will be noticed anyway.

If you have a party favor, make certain it is one that is both memorable and conversational. At a party at Sotheby's to launch internationally known photographer Norman Parkinson's book, *Fifty Years of Style and Fashion,* the guests loved receiving instamatic cameras as favors and snapped away the evening.

When guests arrive, how they enter as well as how they leave should be memorable. Having your guests dress in costumes will add to the decor and enhance your theme. They might enjoy a face painter or make-believe tattoos. Supporters like to be engaged in dancing or bidding on a favorite object. You must know when not to overtax them with additional monies. If the tickets to the event are expensive, you don't want to hit them with a cash bar, unimaginative food, a long buffet line, and constant other ploys for funds.

Patriotism is a common chord for all of us. The Challenger Center Gala was moving both because of the tragedy and legacy. Seeing the surviving family members with their children speaking on a video as the concert began really touched everyone.

You can be innovative, but when you take risks you have to think them through. In 1981, at the Museum of Fine Arts Renaissance Evening, economic times were booming in Houston. I decided to take a chance and price the benefactor tables at $10,000 each. This was a first in Houston, as was my million-dollar event. The highest level of contributor was called an honorary host.

As an incentive for the honorary hosts, in addition to preferential seating, their names were printed on the invitation card. Getting the commitment from a $10,000 honorary host meant submitting a proposal before your invitation card actually was sent to the typesetter. This had to be part of the timetable. The honorary hosts dined in a private gallery of the museum the evening of the gala. In an unprecedented example, they were hosted to a dinner at Bayou Bend and received a special commemorative gift. They were met at the entrance to Bayou Bend and taken by carriage to the front door. The honorary hosts first enjoyed cocktails on the Diana Terrace, then adjourned respectively to the Pine, Massachusetts, Empire, and Murphy rooms to dine. Entertainment was provided by the University of Texas at San Antonio Madrigal Group.

In trying to determine table prices, many times it is contingent on the organization and their target audience. With arts organizations such as the museum, ballet, and opera, or some medical causes such as heart and cancer, the high-tariff ticket will work. These table prices range from the $1,500 level to $15,000, with four levels in between. In other situations, there may be only two levels of support. For example, the price structuring for tables of ten would be $5,000 and $2,500 (with individual tickets at $500 and $250 per person) or $2,500 and $1,500 (with individual tickets at $250 and $125 per person). The reasoning is that if everyone decides to go for the less expensive level, you can still make your goal if that lesser table is priced accordingly.

I worry about the benefit and fundraising mania that seems to be overtaking not only our city but other cities as well and whether there will be any supporters left. Each group that is out there fundraising needs to develop their loyal supporters that they nurture and bond specifically to their cause. If donors become too scattered in their contributions, all organizations will lose out.

Always bear in mind the present economic conditions and just what the traffic will bear. During the Museum of Fine Arts benefit, if the commemorative Bayou Bend plates hadn't sold, I could have been looking at a lot of plates. I remember Mrs. Alice Brown, a very active member of the Museum of Fine Arts Board and someone I admired, saying when she first heard about the plates, "Well, what will people do with them?" I responded that they could give them as Christmas gifts, place them on a credenza in an office, or buy a set of ten to use as service plates. In creating the idea of the plate, I thought our supporters would receive something for their generous support of the museum. With a door prize ticket, if you don't have the lucky number, you simply lose.

In 1987, when I chaired the "Evening of Hope" benefiting the Bering Community Service Foundation, our goal was to open an AIDS dental clinic. No one wanted to get near anyone with AIDS, and people with HIV were finding it impossible to get dental treatment. The general public didn't know much about AIDS, and they were frightened by their lack of knowledge. The Alley Theater offered us the premiere benefit of *Henceforward,* but we had a problem of where to host the after-party since another play was appearing in the theater facility at the same time. Hearing the news that the lobby space would not be available, I had to let my imagination flow. I looked out the theater manager's office window and said with all the confidence in the world, "Let's do it on Jones Plaza." Mind you, I realized this was a first, and it was going to offer some challenges. Jones Plaza has since become a viable city space featuring weekly entertainment for all of Houston to enjoy.

In planning this event, there were certain considerations, minor and major, that needed attention: Would the Alley playbill have a new cover the evening of the event, and would the theater consider underwriting that cost? For our meetings downtown, would we have office space available? Would our ticket/reservations chairperson be responsible for receiving the ticket orders, depositing the funds, and pulling the tickets for reservations? We also had to look at the theater and determine the different ticket levels.

Twenty of the city's top restaurants did food samplings, art was auctioned, a band played, guests loved being there, and the weather cooperated. As AIDS was not really a popular cause then, and being concerned about security, I had to enlist the support of our local Guardian Angels. Guests attending any function like to know their cars will be parked securely and that they can feel safe. Security in the form of mounted patrol, off-duty patrol, or a group like the Guardian Angels gives guests that sense of well-being.

If you meet an obstacle head on with a bit of optimism, you can turn it around. The word "HOPE" was spelled out on the grass across the street from the theater and was a beacon for our guests. That evening the city was united in support of AIDS research. All of these ideas and concepts will transfer to any city involved in fundraising.

Most people have a fondness for pets. It is a common denominator. When I was asked by my son Kenyon's high school to do a fundraiser for the Episcopal High School Parents Association, the thought of another black-tie event just to be doing a fundraiser made me cringe. As I related my idea of a dog show to the headmaster, I noticed a rather strange expression on his face. He couldn't envision what I meant by the "Canine Follies," which would be an invitational celebrity dog show, carnival, and auction. As they say, the show goes on.

I wanted to do something where the children could participate in the organization and spirit of the event. (Today it is an annual event for the school.) The schedule of activities began with an official welcome from the headmaster, followed by the dog show, barbecue dinner, and auction. Admission prices were $7 per adult and $5 per child, which included the barbecue. The amusement tickets were $10 for twenty-five tickets. The real money, of course, was raised during the auction from the items the parents had secured.

The dog show attracted a variety of entries and sponsors. The categories we created were: YumYum Pooches, owned by well-known restauranteurs; Media and D. J. Hounds, belonging to press and television personalities; Remarkable Rovers; "Dog Eat Dog" Political Pooches; Land Rovers, for real estate moguls; "Putting on the Dog" Dressed-up Dogs; and, of course, the Puppy Love category, for students and the young in years — or young at heart. Every dog received a certificate and award for its best feature, be it the shaggiest coat, brightest smile, or longest tail.

Josh Billings once said, "A dog is the only thing on earth that loves you more than you love yourself." It was in that spirit, combined with the special relationship the children share with their pets, that I wrote Ralston Purina and enlisted them in becoming our annual sponsor. In my proposal to the director of community programs at Ralston Purina, I outlined the event expenses, which included invitations, programs, and rentals such as chairs, tents, and port-o-cans. The response from Ralston Purina was in the form of a $10,000 grant.

In the first year, our budget was $7,500. Our first event raised $50,000, with 1,500 people attending, and we had media coverage from three network affiliate stations. (The second year the money doubled, bringing in $107,000.)

More than 2,500 invitations were sent out, and ninety dogs were expected to participate in the dog show, assuring a good turnout for the auction, carnival, and barbecue.

For our Canine Follies Pooch Master De-tails letter and follow-up correspondence, we used Sparkie, a committee member's dog, and affixed his pawprint to the letters. The De-tails letter informed those with participating pooches of the time to arrive, which was forty-five minutes before they were supposed to appear. A map was attached showing which gate to enter the campus and how to find the designated celebrity parking area. A color-coded registration canine station and our canine sitters were ready and waiting to look after the beloved pooches until showtime.

In the event of rain, a school setting such as the gymnasium, school cafeteria, or a covered patio offers great options. This is a comforting thought to place in the back of one's mind.

One of the main positives about an event like this is the involvement of the students. Not only did the students volunteer for the pooper-scoop detail, but they volunteered to be canine cuddlers and helpers in general. Students brought pictures of their own pooches to show so that their classmates could help in the selection process (we could only accommodate one dog from each class). All of the dog celebrities had credits in the program and were given fun snacks. Students were given the opportunity to dunk some of their favorite and unfavorite teachers in the schoolground entertainment.

This was an event where children, families, and faculty worked together for the school. The event had a nice feeling and was well received. Usually in a school setting there will be a student whose parent is in the restaurant business and will work with you on the catering. We were fortunate that restauranteur Jim Goode, world-famous for his barbecue, had children in school and is still participating.

The pre-party, Paw Print Preview, took sheer guts on my part. The party was held poolside at the Ritz-Carlton Hotel. Believe it or not, there was no aggressive behavior on the part of the dogs or their owners, and everything came off without a hitch. The dogs even took a dip in the pool. My son Kenyon's faithful golden retriever, Charlie, who normally welcomes all the guests at our home, had been given shots and had to miss the party.

Shara Fryer, a news anchor for Houston's Channel 13, had her golden retriever, Brute, on hand. When Zachary, the Weimaraner, met Brute, they plunged into the pool like a pair of synchronized swimmers. There is some advantage to coming to a party like this in a pickup truck or station wagon, knowing you might leave with a very wet dog. A couture buyer from Sakowitz brought his Afghan hound, Pasha, decked out with a bib of jewels. Can you imagine Channel 13's nationally known white knight crusader Marvin Zindler and his teacup poodle, Cozy?

Many events have been spawned by the Canine Follies. There are style shows today with celebrity pooches not to be outdone by their masters or mistresses. People love to show off their pets, especially for a good cause. The original concept of Canine Follies is still working as a Field Day event involving children and parents. It takes place on campus, while the auction is separate and held off campus.

A contribution is made by the school through the efforts of the students to a deserving animal rights organization, such as the SPCA, the Stevens and Pruett Humane Ranch, or an organization that finds homes for retired greyhounds. The Field Day still highlights the dog show and includes crafts, basketball shoots, shoe scrambles, tug of war bouts, and relay races. In February of 1993, the auction raised $473,198, making it one of the most successful held by a private school.

The diversity of the ideas and the people who take part keep renewing my enthusiasm. Literally, from event to event, you go from the doghouse to the penthouse.

So often the basic details in planning an event require creative approaches. Such was the case when Marvin Hamlisch and I shared the dream of raising $1 million for the Stehlin Foundation for Cancer Research.

Marvin and I began planning about who we would like to appear and their availability, as the stars would have to not only donate their talent but make a firm commitment to a certain date. Because Dr. Lu Katzman had been a cancer patient of Dr. Stehlin, her close friend, the multi-talented actress/performer Ann Margret, agreed to attend. Liza Minnelli, a childhood friend of Marvin's, committed early on to be a part of the evening. Alan King and Crystal Gayle completed the all-star lineup.

We needed a host hotel to provide accommodations for our star performers and to underwrite the after-party with the stars for our big-ticket purchasers. As good fortune would have it, I was seated at a dinner next to Isadore Sharp, the owner of the Four Seasons Hotel. In conversation, I learned he had lost someone very close to him and his family to cancer. We began talking and I told him of the project Marvin Hamlisch and I were working on for the Stehlin Foundation. I asked him if he would like to meet Dr. Stehlin and tour the laboratory at St. Joseph's Hospital. There was our beginning. Getting the airline transportation underwritten, arranged, and coordinated for our stars was another step. Rehearsal times had to be organized with the Houston Symphony Orchestra.

It was like orchestrating two separate events, as careful attention had to be given to the after-party for our major benefactors and the stars. The performers needed to be entertained and thanked for their generous donation of talent, energy, and time, and our high-ticket buyers would love being in the company and close proximity of the stars at the more intimate Midnight Supper Dance with the Stars.

Limousines had to be arranged for our celebrity transportation to and from the airport and, of course, the stars all had different arrival and departure schedules. I remember one limousine company owner willing to provide limousines galore for a signed Cloris Leachman photograph for his celebrity wall. You can see the potential here for becoming a world-class negotiator. I'm not going to tell you securing that autograph was easy. For a moment, if all else failed, I was prepared to sign her photograph myself.

How do you begin to sell those tickets, to market that evening? There is a hidden energy that has to be there for something to take off. You can feel it but can't see it. Column drops or publicity releases can help build excitement leading up to the event. Of course, those stars had such great appeal that this was a natural in selling tickets. Public service announcements with a telephone number were aired frequently on the local television stations.

Dr. Stehlin and I appeared on any and every talk show or radio interview that would invite us in order to hype the event. Being a guest on the local CBS affiliate morning show meant being there by 5:30 A.M. A fundraiser has to be willing to make such a sacrifice. You never know who will be in the listening or viewing audience. I get calls and faxes all the time from people wanting to be involved. Many times they can't support the event with funds but want to help.

I had to constantly think of ways to generate story ideas to present to the media. The focus would be Dr. Stehlin, a successful patient story, new advances in the treatment of cancer, and news items on stars who would perform and celebrities who would attend.

Dr. Stehlin's nude mice are rather famous in the medical world. We took medical television reporters by to talk with research doctors about the projects they were currently working on. The reporters visited patients in the Living Room at St. Joseph's, where the philosophy of treating the patient as well as the cancer abounded. Anyone walking past the Living Room on an afternoon in late October of that year heard strains of "The Way We Were," "Tomorrow" and "What I Did For Love." That was the day Marvin Hamlisch stopped by and left an enthusiastic crowd of patients and hospital staff with songs in their hearts and smiles on their lips.

There are occasions when I have been asked to offer advice on fundraising projects. I had the pleasure of visiting with actress Shirley Knight when she was performing in Edward Albee's *Marriage Play* at the Alley Theater. A friend invited me to join them for lunch to talk about how she might raise funds for the American Film Institute. Shirley was one of twelve women selected to make a thirty-minute film budgeted at $5,000 each. She felt that she and another awardee, author Rita Mae Brown, would be able to raise their funding but was not certain that it would be as easy for the others.

It was interesting to discuss different ideas to raise the needed $60,000 to fund the project for all twelve recipients, or at least have a reserve for those needing assistance. Considering the fact that all twelve were women, individuals like Frances Lear and her publication came immediately to mind. So did the Virginia Slims group, which sponsors the tournament for women tennis pros. The money could be raised by a total commitment from a corporation or parceled into smaller increments from individuals. This type of brainstorming and networking is part of the fun of being a fundraiser. It is like trying to solve a puzzle and finding the right piece to fit. Shirley's lovely parting words were, "My two best friends are Joanne Woodward and Erica Jong. Let me know if we can ever be of help."

I met Pam Peabody through a mutual friend and she was already working on a film about the artist Dorothy Hood. Pam previously had been recognized for a film called *The Female Line*. This was a documentary on three generations of women in the Peabody family, namely Mrs. Malcolm Peabody, a civil rights activist, Marietta Tree, former United Nations ambassador, and Frances Fitzgerald, Pulitizer Prize author. These women were Pam's well-known Massachusetts in-laws.

Dorothy Hood has exhibited in many prestigious galleries and is in twenty-eight permanent collections, including the Whitney Museum and the Modern Museum of Art in New York and the National Gallery in Washington, D.C. She is a celebrated artist in our city and might be considered a cult heroine. Her paintings reveal both her strength and mysticism. She always seeks the truth and holds a deep reverence for artists of the past.

The self-portrait film would be called *Dorothy Hood: The Color of Life*. It would be a 16-millimeter, half-hour color documentary available for public television, cable, museum, school and public library markets. KUHT, Channel 8 in Houston, was committed to air the film in Texas and offer it to the 270 public television stations around the country.

Pam selected Carl Colby to direct the film. She had seen a film he did on the artist Franz Kline on PBS and thought he had the sensitivity needed to capture Dorothy. Pam had met an impasse in raising the funding for the film and felt that she needed me to help her finish the project. I then became the catalyst that pushed the project ahead by helping someone who had come to my city and wanted to make a film about an artist and the work she loved. My working title on the film was associate producer.

Pam has a great sense of humor and jokingly said that although she loved making a film about an artist, she vowed never to do so again — at least, not one about a living artist. She was like the new kid in town and experienced a resistance in raising the money because she was an out-of-towner. The backlash occurred because at that time so many people were coming to Houston to raise money and were taking the funds to be used elsewhere.

Pam had no choice but to come here to Dorothy's turf to fundraise. It was difficult to try to do that on her own ground in Washington, since, as you can well imagine, Washington is oversaturated with fundraising causes for innumerable projects. She already had $97,000 committed to the project, $70,000 of that from a patron of Dorothy's. The film was budgeted at $150,000. Transportation for the crew and film production costs were some of the main items in the budget. Continental Airlines provided the air transportation for the segment that would be shot in Mexico. It was important to capture Dorothy in the atmosphere that influenced her life and art forever.

The logical support group for the film would have been art patrons who owned Dorothy's work. However, a list of Dorothy's patrons was not made available to us, so we had to try to figure out who they were. That group would have been the natural choice to want to support a film about an artist whose work they admired and collected. In the correspondence I sent out on the project, a letterhead was printed with a list of the prestigious people already committed to the project. I hoped this would inspire others to become involved. Because I believed in Dorothy, art education, and the importance of films like this being made, I set out on this fundraising odyssey.

We began an extensive letter-writing campaign to corporate supporters and people with a proclivity for giving to art and film-related projects. This targeted a certain profile of a supporter. Potential supporters were invited to an event at a local restaurant, where the producer, associate producer, artist, and director were introduced to discuss the project. We hosted a series of small gatherings both in Houston and in Washington, and were able to get media exposure in the social and art sections in both cities' newspapers.

Our strongest selling point was the artist, Dorothy Hood, who had an interesting story to tell. The twenty-eight-minute film is a poignant self-portrait of Dorothy, utilizing still photographs of her as a young girl with her family. Her early talent in drawing, which later evolved into her abstract expressionist style, won her a scholarship at the Rhode Island School of Design.

One of Dorothy's paintings, *Halley's Worlds Diptych 1985,* a large oil on canvas, was used as the invitational cover for the film premiere to be shown at the Museum of Fine Arts as well as the Corcoran Gallery in Washington, D.C. Many corporations participated in the funding, and all the contributors were listed in the credits at the end of the film. A reception following the film premiere in both cities honored our supporters.

When you see a film about an artist, you appreciate their art all the more. Knowing what came before in their lives and what is happening now is not that far apart. The film gives more people, in all parts of the country, the opportunity to know artists like Dorothy Hood. She has been an inspiration to young artists in the Southwest and will influence those who see the film about her life.

We were thrilled when the film was recognized at the American Film and Video Festival, the most respected festival for documentaries, in 1987. It has been shown in eleven major cities across the continent.

CHAPTER 4

Pre-planning

Once you have selected your theme and other relevant information, it is time to write and issue a press release. This initial press release needs to be updated as the fundraising campaign progresses in order to pique everyone's interest.

If someone on the committee has a flair for writing, or even if it takes the combined effort of the executive director of the agency and the chairperson, encourage them to put together a straightforward story about the event. A "for information" phone number included in the write-up will get response. This will encourage people who want to become involved and let them know where and how to respond.

You can prepare a press release within your own group. Who knows better about a disease, its status, the research available, or any significant strides to fight it than the people involved in the event?

It is important to share as much information as possible with the public. Make up a list of your daily newspapers, weeklies, monthlies, and local magazines. Find out the appropriate person to speak with at each publication and set up an appointment. Usually the publication will direct you to the person you need to contact. For example, at Cornell Media I spoke with the publisher. The group publishes several Houston monthly magazines and agreed to underwrite our public service announcements if they had space available in their different neighborhood issues.

For the "Evening of Hope" AIDS benefit, the campaign basically had three messages: education, services/programs offered, and the fundraiser. An announcement of the event by the Alley Theater was featured in the *Performing Arts* magazine. Separate media releases went out relating to each message of our campaign in order to provide specific focus.

For the educational information we were hoping to get out to the public, a press conference was held at the dental site location at the Bering United Methodist Church. Members of the media toured the dental clinic and facilities. There was a question-and-answer session in one of the rooms at the church set up for the press conference. A dentist who was donating his services on a rotating basis, the church pastor, AIDS dental patients, and I answered the media's questions on the programs offered at Bering, medical problems, and facts on the upcoming fundraising event. Announcements and presentations were made to area churches and civic organizations. The publicity was slated to begin in early August, prior to the invitations being dropped in the mail at the end of August.

Letters were written to the food editors at both local papers, in the hope that they would feature some of the restaurants that were donating the food samplings for the post celebration. You couldn't imagine a more wonderful menu created by twenty of the city's top restaurants. Items included Bertha's famous empanadas and margaritas; amaretto and chocolate cheesecakes from How Sweet It Is; Brennan's world-famous bananas foster; an oyster bar from one of the great seafood restaurants; smoked filet of beef with tomato relish; roasted leg of lamb with thyme and red wine sauce; and miniature pizzas. I had asked each of the chefs to create a chef's hat that related to the particular food they were featuring. They were very creative, and a winner was proclaimed. Shades of Carmen Miranda!

The party on Jones Plaza required coordinating the rental services and the electrical people to determine the needs of each food donor. An overall map of the plaza was planned so that the chefs would know where their food stations were being set up.

You are never assured that the media will take your information and go forward. Remember, there are many other organizations vying for space to communicate their messages. Your group will definitely stand out from the crowd if you hand-deliver your information to the publication. The personal hands-on involvement will show the commitment you and your group feel. The newsworthy event could be the opening of a clinic for neurofibromatosis patients, the ribbon-cutting ceremony of the Thomas Street Center (an outpatient clinic for patients with AIDS), a kickoff launching a significant fundraising effort such as a telethon or concert, or a celebrity lending his or her support to an anti-drug rally.

If the cause you are presenting has credibility, then the press may lend a hand to be supportive and help you reach a broader public base. You will gain a sense of accomplishment when you take your fundraiser through all the processes. Making things happen is part of the fulfillment for me. If you are successful and received coverage for your event, a note or follow-up telephone call will be appreciated. No one likes to be taken for granted, especially the media.

As the time of the event arrives, be certain to send an invitation to the media with whom you have had contact and follow up with a telephone call to see if they plan to attend. If they are, you should ask if they will be alone or if they require two seats. Are they bringing a photographer and will he or she need to be seated? When photographers are working, they usually don't want to sit.

When media representatives check in at the reception desk, a press kit, if available, should be put aside for them. The press kit should be nicely presented in a folder with the organization's logo, information on the organization and its nonprofit status, copies of any press that has been received during the campaign, a schedule of event activities, seating and assignment chart, guest list, and contact person. Be certain to invite reporters from all newspapers so that you are not showing favoritism. It is a good idea to seat the media with someone directly involved in your organization, an honored guest, or a visiting celebrated person.

There will be occasions when your group has to supply a photographer. If this is the case, you have to assign a committee member who has been involved with the event to show the media person around. After all, you do want them to be aware of and acknowledge key people involved in the effort and planning of the fundraiser. Newspapers work on a deadline. You have to work closely with the photographer to make certain the press gets the contact sheets or photographs on schedule.

Although your cause may be uppermost in your mind, remember that the press is constantly meeting everyone else's deadlines.

Try to have your press release and photographs when and where they want them. It is important to identify people, left to right, on the backs of the photographs. Try to be as professional as you can. This will encourage the media to work with your group again. Most newspapers prefer casual poses shot in black and white, with subjects looking away from the camera. However, if the photographer shoots in color film, it can be printed in black and white.

If you are working by my zero-budget formula, you can request that the newspapers send the photographs back. Be sure to include a self-addressed envelope and a note asking the media to return your photographs. This doesn't mean you will get the photographs back, but it is worth the effort. If you do, you can recycle to another publication or send the photos to those in the pictures. People appreciate a thoughtful follow-up remembrance.

The more experience you gain, the more your confidence will grow and the more you will develop your own feel in working with the media.

Also essential to the planning of an event is the design of the invitation card. You should recognize the underwriters, patrons, and sponsors. This is your opportunity to thank those generous in-kind donors who make the contributions of food, spirits, music and printing that enable you to create miracles. Besides listing activities of the event, I include speakers as well as supporters in the program to be given out the day of the event. You can never be too appreciative. A thank-you goes long distances.

You will learn to trust your instincts. If a specific country is being honored, you have an entire culture to inspire you. If Mexico is the country, for example, it would be helpful to enlist one of their premier chefs to work with the chef at the location where you are holding the function. The menu should reflect the food and culture of the country that is represented. This would also be interesting information to share with the food editor at your newspaper. A food tasting and preparation of the plates would ensure the overall presentation and success of the dinner. You could invite to your tasting a food editor who might consider writing an article on the cuisine.

At a consular dinner, for example, you could have your silent auction items displayed in a separate room from the main ballroom during the cocktail hour preceding dinner. If you have them in the same room as the ballroom, they will lose their importance. It is a good idea to include silent auction items from the country that is being honored. Show off that country's best in needlepoint, silver, leather goods, art, crafts, or any other items for which their particular country is recognized. If you have a volunteer group available, such as the Houston Jaycees, perhaps they can supply bid runners who will keep the person who has cast the last current bid abreast of his or her latest competition.

Music makes a cocktail reception lively. Libations can reflect the culture of the country. It might be interesting to name the tables in the main room after the famous cultural and artistic heroes and heroines of that particular country.

Another suggestion is to have someone carry the flag of each of the larger cities dressed in costume appropriate to that city at either the opening or closing portion of the program. As a romantic teenager, I have memories of the Villa Fontana in Mexico City and their famous violinists, who would stroll through a dining room in marvelous costumes and serenade everyone with their sweeping, glorious sound. Your selection of an orchestra could have a Latin influence. In Spain, the flamenco is a featured dance. In Mexico, there are many folkloric dancers. All of this tells the story of the country you are representing.

Enlist students such as those from the High School for Performing and Visual Arts or the Alfred C. Glassell Jr., School of Art to work with the gala dinner decorations committee as a class project. They could honor the great Mexican muralists, surrealists, and painters of past and present time.

Look upon this as a great adventure, a history lesson, and a service you are performing. You might even hope to get the president of Mexico or an ambassador to attend, but if not, a special proclamation can be issued by your mayor and the city. Think what fun it would be to have a famous Mexican actor, such as Anthony Quinn, or the opera star Placido Domingo, or one of the country's most popular matadors present at your event. This will become your sparkler.

The favors also should reflect the culture of the country. For the ladies, it could be a marvelous shawl, an exquisite piece of embroidery, or a piece of pottery. The men should have something fun and conversational. How about a sombrero? The pre-party event could focus on a special exhibit by a Mexican artist or sculptor. This could be held at one of the museums that had the exhibit time available, or in a public building space. The wonderful effect is that whatever facility is selected will benefit from the event at the same time that the organization is recognized.

To commemorate two of the greatest charters in the world's history of democracy, the French Declaration of the Rights of Man and of the Citizen and our own Bill of Rights, a Texas committee was formed. These documents were approved within thirty days of each other and laid the foundation for guarantees of human rights and democratic government throughout the world. This great historic relationship between America and France made them partners in liberty and maintained a friendship based on mutual respect for freedom.

I chaired the Bill of Rights Committee, whose purpose was to select a Texas artist to commemorate this occasion with an original sculpture to be presented to the city. The budget for the sculpture was determined by the money raised at the Bastille Day Ball celebration and from underwriters who wanted to see this permanent gift presented to the city. Funds were set aside for this purpose. Houston was then focusing on development of the bayou, so our timing was appropriate for the sculpture gift.

My dilemma was how to go about selecting an artist for this commission in a fair manner. At first I thought of a competition, but that can be overwhelming without enough staff to handle sch an effort. The former consul general of France, Gerard Dumont, and I set up an appointment with Mayor Kathryn J. Whitmire to determine if the city would accept the sculpture gift and what our guidelines should be in making the presentation. Mayor Whitmire liked the idea and informed us of the procedure we had to follow to get the sculpture gift accomplished.

The artist was chosen by a selection committee that I established made up of museum directors and twentieth-century art curators from across Texas. I asked Marti Mayo, director of the Blaffer Gallery, to chair the panel selection committee.

Once we had selected an artist, we had to present our idea and obtain the approval of the Municipal Arts Commission (MAC). Sites were then recommended to us for consideration by that commission. After studying and evaluating the several site locations, the artist, Linnea Glatt, and her collaborator, photographer Frances Merritt

Thompson, began to create "Passage Inacheve," which translated means "unfinished journey."

There were several meetings with the city's Parks and Recreation Department during the progress of the work. Many details had to be worked out relating to the space and the exact positioning of the piece. Materials had to be tested to be able to withstand flood water and other elements of nature. The model was approved by the MAC after we submitted samples of the steel, the images in the glass, and the finishes on the concrete floor. Final approval ultimately had to come from the City Council. We kept the public and the supporters abreast of the sculpture progress through press releases to the media. A plaque commemorating the major sponsors was permanently affixed to the work of art.

When the sculpture was completed, I planned a ribbon-cutting ceremony and picnic in the French-style at the site. The pâté and champagne that was offered before the program added to the festive spirit of the day. The champagne was provided by a transplanted Frenchman, Henri Bernabe, who had moved to Texas and created Moyers, an excellent Texas champagne.

The Small Wind Band from the High School for Performing and Visual Arts entertained before and after the ceremony. Flags always add to the international flavor of an occasion like this. You have to use the proper protocol when displaying flags from different countries. The general rule, depending on the country you are in, is that their flag goes on top. This can be confirmed through your local consular offices. You wouldn't want to create a diplomatic incident.

The site, with our spectacular Houston skyline in the background, made one reflect on the view the artist had in mind. It was interesting to watch as joggers and bicyclists rode through the work of art, "Passage Inacheve." This was their new refuge and future contemplative space. According to the artist, Linnea Glatt, the transparent qualities of the sculpture provide a link between the nature of the bayou and the built city beyond. Important to the concept of the sculpture is the idea of human presence. This is expressed by an open framework form suggestive of a shelter, a house, or a room. Seating inside the piece implies a place to sit and reflect. The photographic images, which were taken in France during a visit by Linnea and Frances, speak of man's aspirations, triumphs and freedoms, as well as his struggles and repressions.

The sculpture culminated a year-long celebration of freedom, with the festivities peaking on Bastille Day. Hundreds of bicentennial events took place throughout the United States, featuring dance, art exhibits, plays, trade shows, conferences, symposia, fireworks, films, and displays of new technology.

Helping to keep the public informed is one of the important roles the media plays in the event. Quotes from the new consul general of France, Bernard Guillett, the Texas Committee chairman Dino Nicandros (chairman and CEO of Conoco, Inc.), Mayor Whitmire's office, and my own feelings as chair of the Bill of Rights Committee made up the basic information for a press release. The Office of the Mayor had the responsibility of coordinating the press release on the sculpture dedication. I asked the mayor's assistant chief of staff to organize the information into a press release format that was approved by the parties involved.

I was immensely proud to chair this committee. The symbolism of "Passage Inacheve" is still inspiring today as the concept of freedom spreads throughout the world. We must remember freedom is never permanently secure. It must always be treasured, and, if necessary, defended.

The entire event was videotaped and aired on the Access Cable Network on several occasions. It gave those in the community who did not attend the opportunity to be there, increasing the longevity and awareness of the event. I also used the videotape approach with an AIDS fundraising luncheon, with guest speaker Dr. Matilda Krim, and the neurofibromatosis fundraising event, "My Heart Belongs To Daddy." This reaches even more people, so that the energy you have expended doesn't dissipate and goes even further.

If time allows you to build your momentum before the actual event, two pre-parties can be planned. It is especially nice if an event builds on the energy of past efforts.

One such neurofibromatosis event happened when the A.D. Players, a local theater group, were rehearsing for *The Elephant Man.* Larry Balph, the play's director, saw our film, *This is NF,* produced by Lou Congelio, on the access cable station. He felt Reggie Bibbs, a young man suffering from NF, could really motivate the actors performing in *The Elephant Man.*

Although neurofibromatosis and the "Elephant Man's Disease" are different, they both cause painful disfigurement. NF is a more common genetic disorder causing tumors, however, and certain of these tumors can cause death. The Proteus Syndrome, the disease of the Elephant Man, is very uncommon and can be fatal. Both sufferers are subjected to the cruelty of others from their lack of understanding.

Larry Balph called the Texas Neurofibromatosis office in Dallas and asked how he might contact Reggie. We have always been protective not to let anyone exploit Reggie. After making certain that this would be something Reggie would want to do, Larry picked Reggie up and took him to the theater. Larry described how nervous he felt when first meeting Reggie. I knew what he meant, as I had that same feeling at our first meeting at M.D. Anderson Hospital. The actors were so moved and inspired by Reggie that they decided to give an extra benefit performance. I thought it only appropriate that we dedicate the performance to Reggie. The director said the actress in the play, who befriended the Elephant Man, was a philanthropist as well. The actors sometimes called her Carolyn Farb during rehearsals. Talk about walking on a cloud!

It is important to encourage people with the disease to become involved. This has been a form of therapy for Reggie which has strengthened his self-image. The primary focus when fundraising should always be on the worthy cause you are supporting.

For example, a young woman I sat with during a luncheon for the Austrian ambassador's wife had been battling the disease lupus for some time. She had been relentless in trying to seek out doctors, treatment, and information all over the country. I encouraged her to become a spokesperson for lupus, which is not that common. In doing so, her role became a positive one of helping others. Prior to her illness, and still, she has been an active member of the community. I am delighted to say that by speaking out on behalf of her disease, she made an impact on the community. She recently chaired a successful fundraiser for lupus research.

Another element in pre-planning is to try to bolster ticket sales. During the Stehlin Foundation campaign, we worked with the fashion section of a newspaper. The story idea was, "How does one look like a million for a Million Dollar Evening?" The article featured how the men could dress for such an evening. It gave them the opportunity to express their individual creative style when dressing black-tie. Instead of wearing the typical tuxedo, some gentlemen coordinated a dinner jacket and contrasting trousers, wore a vest or no vest, a long scarf, or a pocket handkerchief. It was fun to see how the different personalities expressed themselves.

When we were trying to think of ways to get people excited about the Museum of Fine Arts Gala, we had a kickoff party to launch the commemorative plates. The party was hosted by Brennan's Restaurant. There was press coverage about the plate using the Buck Schiwetz drawing of Bayou Bend. The drawing was displayed at each event. In this way, people could see just what the plates would look like. These marketing ideas let the public know when the plates were available.

The poster image that we chose for "A Renaissance Evening" was by the early fifteenth-century Italian artist Bartolommeo Veneto. Poster sales were brisk when they were unveiled at the pre-event held at Tony's Restaurant. In selecting from the collection of the Museum of Fine Arts, Houston, I chose *The Meeting of Solomon and the Queen of Sheba* from the Italian Ferrarese, circa 1470, for the invitation and program. *MFA Today* would drop items to the membership about the upcoming gala evening. Publicity photographs were taken with museum board members and the board chairman dressed in renaissance costumes. Whenever a celebrity-type person such as ball designer Prince Egon Von Furstenberg came to Houston, it created another interesting item.

When you are deciding on a billboard concept, there is usually someone on your fundraising committee with whom you have collaborated on the invitation design, a poster, or event decor. First, you think of what message you are trying to communicate on the billboard. Then you say it in as few words as possible to get the driver's attention in a fraction of time. Seven words or less is considered ideal. The billboard company will help in guiding you through the process of creating a display.

It is becoming more difficult to have public service announcements aired on television because of the deregulation of the broadcast industry. Television and radio stations are not obligated to play your PSA at prime time. More often they will be shown at 3:00 A.M. If you are lucky and have made a good contact with the public service director, your spot may be aired during prime time. The beauty of outdoor advertising is that it is there twenty-four hours a day. The billboard industry in Harris County donates $1.3 million worth of space and materials to nonprofit organizations annually. Patrick Media alone helps more than 200 causes a year.

The image has to make an impact. A well-known personality, logo, eye-catching design, or children with a message are the top attention getters. For the United Cerebral Palsy Starathon '90 campaign, as chairperson I was asked to be featured on the billboard with our poster children, reading together. By chance, I had a dress with a big star on the front reflecting our theme, "Starathon." The same idea was used the following year with the new chairperson and different UCP poster children. Having a chairperson that has community recognition and a previous fundraising track record brings their base of supporters to the cause. The billboard for "An Evening of Hope" featured a group of easily recognized individuals, and the headline stated: "AIDS is everyone's responsibility." I was trying to convey the message that it was okay to support AIDS fundraising. The Jerome Homeless billboard showed a loveable looking pig with the hog hotline number, 523-HOGS.

After you have worked on your artwork with a printer or designer, you then set up an appointment at the billboard company. It is a good idea to allow six to eight weeks from that date. Your non-profit billboard will have to wait its turn behind the paid advertiser. That is one of the important reasons for pre-planning.

During the pre-planning stages for the "Evening of Hope" AIDS benefit, I realized this was going to be an uphill battle with a lot of negatives to overcome. Former Houston mayor Louie Welch had made a remark that later haunted him during his 1985 unsuccessful campaign for mayor. He said, "One way to control AIDS is to shoot the queers." This was picked up by a live microphone from one of the local television stations and spread like wildfire. It was just a thoughtless quip he made that never came from his heart. I knew that he did not mean what he had said; however, I felt it would get everyone's attention if he became involved with our fundraiser. This helped people realize that AIDS is not only a gay issue and that this illness is one toward which people need to be compassionate.

One day I was looking through a magazine and saw a photograph of Elizabeth Taylor, Calvin Klein, and a lot of people who were standing up for people with AIDS. The idea came to me that this was where I would begin to, hopefully, turn the public thinking around in our city.

A local photographer, Ellis Vener, agreed to do the photo shoot. The photograph was taken at the Alley Theater. It involved a cross-section of twenty-eight individuals in our community and included a bishop, artist, ballet dancer, doctors, writers, corporate public relations managers, architects, a former mayor, and community leaders. Mayor Welch joked that I had to subpoena him to be in the photograph. And at the photo session gathering, his presence certainly got everyone's attention.

I began contacting *Texas Monthly*, the *Houston Business Journal*, and other publications to see if they would consider running public service advertisements. Realizing the importance of the cause, they agreed to run our ad if they had space. We had to work out the different ad specifications depending on the space they would have available to donate.

To give you an idea of what you can accomplish in a day and a half, I would like to share our "Breakfast in Bed" vignette. This was created for Desserts and Designs '91 by me and a friend, Pam Giraud, and is the format the organization uses annually as their fundraising vehicle.

All of the proceeds benefited the Hospice at the Texas Medical Center, whose purpose is to provide physical, emotional, and spiritual support to terminally ill people and their families, regardless of their ability to pay. As a special honor and gesture of appreciation, for those who created the room vignettes, a day of hospice care was given in their name.

Our first meeting entailed selecting one of the lobby spaces that had been marked off for the event at the Decorative Center. It was wise to be there on time, as the early bird got what they perceived to be the best location. There would be thirteen sites, and the event featured decadent desserts, music, and cocktails. The furnishings for each vignette would be provided by the different vendors in the Decorative Center or from whatever retailer would loan the desired items.

A lighting specialist was made available the day before the event and the day of the event, as we had to work on the lighting the night before. We could then determine what effect the table lamps and floor lamps we had selected would have with the overall lighting in the entire area.

We chose "Breakfast in Bed" as the theme for our vignette because it sounded racy and fun. Not knowing where to begin and not wanting to begin where everyone else was starting, we headed to The Galleria for our fantasy shopping spree. Initially, we didn't know what type bed we were looking for, but I'm one of those people who knows when I see it. I am committed, however, to make certain I've seen all there is to see before I make the final decision. We found a great bed in the window of an interesting shop called Milieux. Quite by chance, right next to where we found our handsome pencil post bed was another shop called Krispen, with incredible antiques that would provide the proper eclectic mix. All I had to do was convince the stores how much participating in this event could mean to them as far as new business. Both stores were in a remote location at The Galleria, and if you didn't know where to go, you might not find them.

We continued to embellish our loosely defined Southwestern theme with all of the accoutrements that would create the perfect bedroom for a gentleman in the outback. How about a water buffalo coat rack, a stub zebra painting, large tortoise shell, Ralph Lauren bed linens, Dhurrie rug, monkey screen, croquette mallet, old golf clubs, cowboy hat, duster, and a collection of antique walking sticks? Have you got the picture?

What really set our vignette apart from the others were the two handsome men wearing burgundy-colored Ralph Lauren robes who alternated schedules and enjoyed breakfast in bed while reading the financial news. You might ask, where would I find two such bold and brave volunteers? The thought of Chippendales came to mind and another illustrious spot that I have never been to called La Bare. I decided to take the coward's way out.

I called a monthly publication called *Houston Health and Fitness* magazine and asked my friend the editor, Diane Stafford, if she had any ideas where we could find some men who could compete with the decadent desserts. There was a long pause before she said that she was looking at a candidate in her office as we spoke. Our first recruit was a member of her office staff who was seriously into fitness and didn't mind showing off his pecs. The other needed more convincing, as he was a stockbroker with a rather staid firm. He didn't know how that would sit with his conservative image. Pam and I invited both gentlemen to lunch and, good sports that they were, they agreed to join my growing list of IOUs.

As each perfect gentleman sipped his champagne, tasted strawberries and cream, and read the *Wall Street Journal* and *Forbes,* the more than 500 guests passed by. I must confess, we created a traffic jam as the guests lingered and swooned. The Gene Autry songs of the Old West playing in the background added the perfect nostalgic touch. On the day we set up, it was an option to pass through the many wonderful shops in the Decorative Center to add those finishing touches to the vignette. We wanted everything.

The kickoff party for the Art League of Houston's Gala Metalmorphosis was held at a nightclub. In keeping with our theme of molten metal, since we were honoring sculptor Charles Pebworth, the metal fashions by Anthony Ferrara, known as the king of metal, were a great match. It was almost like serendipity to honor a metal sculptor with a metal fashion show. This was the prelude for the Art League gala that honored Charles Pebworth as the Texas Artist of the Year.

The Art League is a nonprofit organization that has promoted visual arts in Houston for more than thirty-eight years. Its roots go back to 1900, with the founding of the public school art league by Miss Emma Richardson Cherry. The charge at the time was to put five paintings in each public school classroom so that the children of Houston would know more about culture.

The Art League holds a unique place in the city as a truly democratic nonprofit organization. It also functions as an alternative space where artists can exhibit their work. Its members include the vast majority of Houston's full-time artists, as well as teachers, students, art patrons, and friends of the visual arts from all walks of life. This shows how a network with artisans of all types can globally come together. Its influence outside of Houston is a computerized registry of visual artists, the only resource of its kind in Texas.

Many local artists, including Jim Love, Earl Staley, Jack Boynton, James Surls, and Dan Allison, donated works to the auction that began the gala evening. The sumptuous dinner, serving samples of several ethnic cuisines, took us through the various stages of molten metal, beginning with its natural state. As the hot evening began to cool down, nothing was cooler than dancing to the special orchestra of the evening, Big Rockin' Dopsey and the Twisters. This funky Zydeco sound was featured on Paul Simon's *Graceland* album. The centerpieces, each one a unique clay habitat made by artist Andrea Badner, were purchased by guests to add to the coffers. I still use mine with a votive candle inside when entertaining outdoors, and they serve as a wonderful memento from the evening.

Just like major business projects, major fundraising events require a significant lead time and very thorough pre-planning. Many preparatory events need to happen along the way to make the main event successful. Building the initial team of volunteers, receiving publicity by early press interaction, scheduling billboard publicity and kick-off meetings, planning videotape and advertising, scheduling celebrities, and selecting the event location are but a few of the major pre-planning requirements. Listing all of the required action items with a beginning and a completion date early in the pre-planning process is essential in order not to be surprised by scheduling conflicts or late relative to critical deadlines. Forming a project team early on and working regularly as a team is a major help in effective pre-planning.

CHAPTER 5

Organization

Apriceless asset for any fundraiser is a mailing list of prospects who will support your cause. This is to the event what maps and a supply line are to an invading army.

What if you have an organization that is just beginning? You start creating a mailing list name by name, company by company, and foundations in the same manner. A list of foundations can be obtained from the School of Public Affairs of a university or through your state government. The listing will describe the type of foundation, the focus of its support, when and how often it meets, and who is on the board.

Some of the individuals coming together in support of a particular charity or community effort will have names to add to a mailing list, including doctors, if it is a medical cause. Museums and other nonprofit groups such as the symphony, the ballet, and performing arts groups will have a built-in base of followers—many who are subscribers and guild members. The goal of any organization is to continually expand that database and to identify and hold on to a specific target audience for that group. Once you have become involved with a group, you can focus whenever you are out in public. You should collect business cards of people you meet, save invitations and keep programs of events and concerts. Read the local newspapers and those in other cities when you are away for more ideas. In the business and social sections, you will find the names of community-spirited individuals and corporations to add to your rolodex.

The core of your mailing list can begin with attendees and contributors to a past event. Immediately after the last fundraiser, you should always start adding to your mailing list. You can network with corporate individuals and other professionals on an ongoing basis through your job contacts. Once your list takes shape, you will have to decide whether the contribution will be a personal or a corporate one. This will determine to which address the correspondence is mailed and also where you will direct any follow-up calls.

No matter how thorough your mailing list is, someone is always left off. This is when you have to do some personal networking. Volunteers can make a person-to-person telephone push, canvassing friends and associates to buy tickets. The main objective when you are having an event is that people not only purchase tickets but actually attend. You don't want a half-empty hall. If supporters can't use their tickets, encourage them to give the tickets to friends. If they don't want to bother finding someone, tickets can be turned back in to be resold or given to deserving campaign volunteers.

For the volunteers involved in the theater tickets sales for the "Evening of Hope," there were certain proposed procedures. The order forms were separated by the type of payment, such as credit card, cash, or personal check. The information on each ticket purchased was filed only after the information had been entered into a computerized list.

It was important to set a deadline to print the completed list so that the seating was on a first-come, first-served basis. Tickets were then mailed out the week of September 18–25. All of these details had to be finely tuned so that the seating would flow smoothly. None of us had ever done this before, so we had to devise our own system with the backup assistance of the Alley Theater. To make the process of stuffing the envelopes fun, a party was organized at the Bering United Methodist Church. A calendar of significant dates is a good way to let your volunteers know what is expected of them and their timetable. This is most helpful to volunteers with a specific assignment, such as ticket sales.

When high-ticket sales appear soft or need a boost, an approach that is helpful is to offer incentives to those high-ticket purchasers. During the "Evening of Hope" AIDS benefit, a framed lithograph donated by artists Jack Boynton and Trudy Sween was a perk. An invitation to a post-event brunch with Piper Laurie, the star of the Alley Theater's other play, *The Last Flapper*, was offered to those who purchased sponsorship tickets. When you don't have a built-in support group, these are some remedies to bolster ticket sales.

Because of the many requests for funding within corporations, development directors, heads of human resource departments, or members of an executive contributions community have to decide whether or not they can support your cause. You should not be disillusioned if you are not granted a request the first time. Most have a budget from the previous year, and it may take time before your worthy cause is given funding consideration. At least you have made an initial pitch. When they receive a written proposal, they will have some knowledge and be informed of the cause or group. If your organization receives good press, or an interesting article is written, you should send it to the head of that funding committee or someone you know on the board.

When you are sending a pre-invitation letter, asking for early benefactor support, some form of personalization may make a difference. Initial fundraising campaign letters should always cover who, what, why, where, how, and when. Your hope is that the request gets beyond its first barrier and is not put into the infamous File 13. The letter you are writing to raise funds is a direct communication between two people, so it should be warm and sincere. You have to appeal to the recipient on several levels. Some may give because they want to be supportive of your efforts. Some are simply compassionate, morally inspired to do the right thing, interested in changing the world, or needing to feel better about themselves.

It always gives an extra boost to someone receiving correspondence if they recognize a name on the letterhead. This is especially true when the cause is not well-known and doesn't have the same popularity as some other causes. An established chairperson and a list of well-known committee members with proven track records are pluses to spearhead and champion a new cause.

Every letter or piece of correspondence should be well timed. What you are trying to convey should be clear. This is the portion of the campaign that you do in advance to insure that you will have some impressive text to be included into the body of your printed invitation. A description of the disease or statement of purpose will add weight and credibility to your undertaking, coupled with the listing of well-known committee members. Your honorary board of directors, event and honorary chairs, honorees, underwriters, board of directors, executive director, and committee members are names to be listed if space is available.

The response card for a pre-event should be the standard size of a postcard and should have a telephone number. On your response/reservation card for an event you need to include the name of the benefit organization with its logo, as well as the event date and pertinent details. This information is helpful in case the invitation and response card are separated.

Make the different table levels and individual ticket sponsorships clear, and allow a space to be indicated for their choice. Have space available to list names of guests on the reverse side or where requests can be made to be seated with other individuals. Allow a line to show method of payment (by credit card or check). Instructions should be clear regarding to whom checks should be made payable. For credit cards, have space for the number, type of card, expiration date, and signature. The tax-exemption clause should be listed at the bottom of the response card. Specific facts such as day, date, time, location, entertainment, and dress code are standard information. If the event is held at an unusual location, a map or telephone number should be included. This will eliminate confusion and last-minute calling for directions. A limited seating statement will encourage a faster response. It is not necessary to include postage on the response envelope. Although this would be a nice gesture, remember that this is a fundraiser.

It is effective to have letterhead stationery coordinated with the overall theme of your particular event. Try to see if you can have this donated. Whoever is printing the invitations may consider doing the entire job, including stationery, programs, posters, and any other printing needs that arise. Today the public is environmentally conscious, so I try to use recycled paper whenever possible. This relays a message that you are directing all monies to the cause and not to overhead.

In making a pitch to a printer for a donation, if you have knowledge beforehand about their press and the type of work they do it will help in your presentation. A general knowledge of printing terms is practical but not essential. You must be prepared to do some advance work and be flexible to change your design if cost becomes a factor. For example, it may be as simple as going from a three-color design to two. Remember, you have your hat in your hand and are asking for help. Try to be as accommodating, trouble-free, and professional as possible.

Once you and the designer you are working with have built up a comfortable dialogue with the printer, in this great age of technology you can send a computer disk with the information on the artwork or the artwork itself. This was the case with the designer Tom Oddo, who created the boards for "I've Got A Crush On You." A laser proof can be sent on a disk so that the printer will know exactly what your printed material is supposed to look like. When he sees the designer's file, he can match the low-resolution proof with his own negatives.

When you are involved in a fundraising campaign, it is essential to keep an ongoing working dialogue with the executive or development director, head of the board of directors, and the organization's official spokesperson. You need to be able to exchange ideas and thoughts back and forth. The board of directors can direct their energy and sphere of influence to what you are doing, especially when you keep them informed.

I like to share information on the progress of the campaign and give updated reports to board members at their regular meetings. In turn, I welcome their input and involvement. The United Cerebral Palsy board really became excited about the changes we were making in the previous telethon format. Sometimes through the open exchange with the board, you will learn of additional resources that might be helpful.

For example, I needed to talk to someone at the Transco Tower regarding my idea for the drive-through location for the telethon. The husband of a board member was in an executive position with Transco, and he was delighted to run interference for us. Therefore, I was able to find out exactly who I needed to talk with, and we didn't lose any time. It was helpful to touch base with him beforehand so that I could avoid any potential pitfalls and follow the correct path.

Sometimes there are those wonderful situations that happen via serendipity. When I lost my way to an appointment during a fundraising campaign, I stopped to ask for directions. This is how I connected with the Patrick Media Billboard Group. I refer to such timing as seizing the moment. The opportunity was there before me.

Your personal antenna should be receptive to information and questions whenever you have the opportunity.

Once I realized this company might have an interest in our effort, I asked if they ever did public service announcements for nonprofit organizations, and the rest is history. When you have a message to get out to the public, I have found the use of billboards can broaden the audience and raise the level of public awareness.

Neurofibromatosis was practically unheard of, and now through celebrities like Cher, talk shows, and our ongoing research, people are becoming aware and can even pronounce the word. Patrick Media really benefits nonprofit groups who do not have the promotional budget available. Since that fortuitous meeting, I have enlisted their support in several fundraising campaigns. As we geared up for the second neurofibromatosis event, I planned to call on them again.

Your budget is of utmost importance. If you begin with my zero-budget philosophy, it is even more challenging. This will get your creative juices flowing. You might liken this excitement to what a racecar driver feels before a race. There are so many emotions, high and low, that you experience during a fundraising campaign. You have to realize there will be a letdown when it is over. Remember you've been concentrating your energy, focus, and determination into this effort, and it won't be that easy to let go.

Some people believe you have to spend money to raise money. I disagree. One of my best friends, Kathleen Amatangelo, called from Chicago while I was working on this book. She said, "I really appreciate something you shared with me." I said, "Let me get my pad so I can include it in the book." It was about not spending money to raise money. She is working hard to get people to understand the concept. Your corps of volunteers can accomplish a multitude of miracles, such as hemming cloths, creating centerpieces, selling door-prize tickets, addressing envelopes, computerizing mailing lists, passing out literature, manning hot lines, and creating items for fundraising.

Recently I visited our first NF camp session in Kerrville, Texas. It was a gathering for NF families in rustic surroundings that encouraged the sharing of common problems and solutions. As I roamed through the camp, I became intrigued with two women standing side by side in the craft area. The identical location of their facial tumors and the genetic character of NF led me to assume they were mother and daughter. This was not the case; they were two patients with NF. Still, for an instant, the cruel nature of the disease hit home.

The elder of the two was busy painting crushed cans that had been shaped into animals and little people and attached to grapevine wreaths. My mind began racing with creative possibilities. How could I involve patients and volunteers in a fundraising project creating wreaths for seasonal occasions? Once I was back in Houston, I had to reflect on how to make the dream happen. First, I consulted with Jan Griffin, the woman from the camp, and the Texas NF executive director, Bob Hopkins, to present my plan. As Jan lived in a small town near Dallas, this meant she would have to travel to Houston and the other NF offices to teach volunteer groups her wreath-making process. Privately, I wondered if the volunteers could actually recreate Jan's designs. One of the main reasons it has worked is because of the deep commitment of our volunteers.

In thinking through the concept, we decided that wreaths are friendly and could be appropriate for any occasion. The motif could be varied seasonally to include designs for fall, Halloween, Christmas, Valentine's Day, football games, livestock events, and Easter, to mention a few possibilities.

The next step was to arrive at a marketing plan. We had to consider where we could purchase the materials at the most cost-efficient price. Many shows where items such as wreaths could be sold charge an exhibitor's fee for the booth. Fortunately, for our first venture, many of the nonprofit organizations I had worked with in the past welcomed the new endeavor. The Harris County Medical Auxiliary agreed to waive their exhibitor's fee in respect of our nonprofit status. We were given a booth near the front entrance to their Christmas show. When you have items priced at $30 and $40, you have to sell a lot of goods to justify an exhibitor's booth that can have an entry fee ranging from $600 to $1,200.

There were other ways to market the wreaths, such as having samples on display in gift shops like the one at M.D. Anderson Cancer Center, with a number to call to place an order. Church and school bazaars generally charge nominal fees. Your group can piggyback with another group and share a space when you are just beginning your project. This is helpful when your inventory has not been built up and taking orders is more efficient. Samples of what you are selling can be shown in a color catalogue or brochure. Order forms should be provided and delivery arranged with a charge included for the delivery and packaging service. Your project can be given momentum through word of mouth, and before you realize it, the items will be in great demand. Displaying items at beauty salons, shoe repair shops, or local dry goods cleaners can generate prospective buyers for your worthwhile cause. Operation Wreath is currently working to meet the demands.

Every event will dictate its own expense needs and the items that must be purchased. The bottom line is that you will have to analyze the items and services that you can get underwritten and assess those you cannot get donated. You should make a list of real expenses and donated items and services that you will add or delete as you move further along in the process.

Your income and revenue will come from the efforts you apply to underwriters, table and individual ticket sales, auction proceeds, contributions from supporters unable to attend, and any ad or program sales. The expenses will vary according to how much you can get donated. It will depend on the specific event and other variables.

Some of the fixed expenditures that you may not be able to get donated include food and beverages, catering, entertainment, special requirements such as audio-visual, lights and sound, postage and express mail, insurance, and photographer/photos. Although it may be easy to write a check, it is far more challenging to use your imagination to turn these potential expenses into donated items.

There are always new businesses that love the idea of associating with worthwhile causes and civic endeavors. This presents a positive image for them in the community. These new business contacts might include florists, local and national corporations, jewelers, retailers, foundations of celebrities, grocery chains, restaurants, wholesale wine and liquor distributors, advertising agencies, and printing companies. The key is to avoid burnout by not always asking the same individuals or companies, but to be adventurous and seek new contracts.

You can brainstorm by looking at new stores in shopping centers and malls. You can keep current by reading the business section of your local papers, *The New York Times,* and *The Wall Street Journal* to learn what is going on in your community and who is coming to your city. Many times the people you have already involved with your event in the past will be offended if they are not included each and every time. It becomes their cause, their way of giving of themselves.

If you are using a hotel as the setting for the event, there are items that cannot be underwritten. You should always try to negotiate the best on expenses, cutting back here and there with the banquet manager for your nonprofit organization. When I was at a planning meeting with the Hyatt Hotel general manager, Tom Netting, for UCP's Starathon '90 victory party, he surprised me by donating, from his own collection, two very coveted signed basketballs for our pre-party event called Sportsmania. Those are priceless items that are so difficult to secure that this seemed like serendipity.

Remember, in negotiating you have some leverage as these fundraising events generate revenue and recognition for the hotel as well. The better the job they do, the more other organizations will want to use their facilities for upcoming events. Generally, it is a give-and-take relationship and works well for both parties.

The hotel management may make consideration such as free hotel accommodations for out-of-town celebrities and dignitaries. Perhaps they will consider hosting a special breakfast, luncheon the next day, or food-tasting prior to the event as a thank-you for a limited number of the committee members and out-of-town guests. If you order wine, they may offer to only charge a corking fee. This doesn't always work out to your advantage, as you are usually hopeful of getting your wine donated or at a very special price. Sometimes they may underwrite the valet parking for your guests to give your event a special touch.

There are many options you need to be aware of and consider. The hotel may have props, centerpieces or candelabras in storage that they can loan, which will add to your event. In selecting your food, remember your supporters are not expecting a Chaine de Rotisseur menu, and they will respect a conservative choice rather than an extravagant one. If it is too pricey, they will wonder how the cause will receive the benefit. Offer either a red or white wine, not both. This is a subtle way of saving and budgeting. The cocktail reception should run forty-five minutes gratis, then it is appropriate to switch to a cash bar when dinner and wine are being offered. This is your responsibility to monitor when you are at the helm and have specific dollar goals you are trying to reach.

In hiring an orchestra, be open. You may discover new and exciting local talent right in your own city. Usually a group that is relatively unknown will consider donating their services for the exposure that can lead to other paid engagements. Gather a group of your committee members to help you do what I call music research.

If you aren't planning a fundraiser and like the sound of a group you hear, take their card for future reference. If they aren't able to play at your event, maybe they will know someone who can. This is a way to network. In this way, if you contact a group directly it will be less expensive than involving the group's manager or booking agent. It is always worth a try. Music adds so much to any event. I try to always include it during the reception hour, where guests get to mingle. This is their opportunity to see and be seen, and they enjoy this freedom to circulate. Once you are seated, you don't have that freedom to move around as much.

In our city, we have the High School for Performing and Visual Arts as well as the renowned Shepherd School of Music at Rice University. Often these outstanding learning institutions are great sources of talent and will donate jazz, chamber, and marching band ensembles for a particular event such as the Challenger Gala. This gives their students the opportunity for practical experience and showcases the cultural resources of our city. This is, of course, dependent on the schedule of the school and of the students. At Christmas time, the Shepherd School Bell Choir adds the perfect touch to a holiday gathering. They appreciate a contribution to their organization as well, but are usually happy to play for gratis if they feel the cause or organization is worthwhile.

If you find a group of volunteers that work well together, you'll want to use them again for future events. I have a group of regulars that are literally waiting and ready to go on the next project.

We turn volunteerism into a good time, and in turn what we are doing makes us feel good. There is a mutual respect that must exist between everyone. I try to always be considerate of everyone's time. In being aware of this, my famous manifesto has come into play. Each individual knows where the buck stops. They appreciate knowing just what commitment is expected of them in advance so that they can plan ahead. We usually have meetings at the site so that everyone will fully understand the logistics and have a feel for the space. This is another way my hands-on philosophy manifests itself. In this way, volunteers will be totally informed and helpful to the guests in case of the unexpected circumstance and will feel comfortable with the entire effort.

I was delighted to be asked to serve on the Economic Summit Host Committee. An advertising agency came up with our slogan, "Houston's Hot," for the city. This is obvious if you have ever visited Houston in the summer, especially in August. I thought we needed to take the slogan a step further and designed a fan in the shape of the city skyline. It was the type of fan on a wooden stick that you may have seen in churches before air-conditioning. Printed on the back of the fan were all the wonderful, positive reasons why Houston is hot. The skyline was the cutout of the top portion. This was given to all of our visiting press, foreign visitors, and citizens who were a part of the effort. There wasn't time to find a corporate sponsor, so I decided to make it my gift to the city. This is another example of how you will be motivated to take charge, when your feelings are strong. Ironically, the Houston Hot fans became the most sought after souvenir of the Economic Summit.

One of the four entertainment venues for the Houston Economic Summit International press party was at the Menil Collection. This entailed a tremendous amount of overall coordination, from the moment our press visitors stepped off their buses, stop number one, until they got back on to go to the next venue. We knew we were creating a worldwide impression of our city. This gave our multilingual volunteers the opportunity to shine and be important members of the team in greeting our international guests.

As I mentioned in Chapter 2, with the Change, Inc. Foundation benefit at Barney's our supporters would be going to two venues: the first at the new Barney's New York in The Galleria, followed by the opening of Robert Rauschenberg's art exhibit and after-party at the Menil Collection. This was complicated, but not impossible. One of my goals was to make the move for our guests as effortless as possible. As the event began in early evening, most of the guests preferred the option of going home to change before attending the Barney's New York opening at The Galleria. Valet parking was kept at a minimum. I didn't want them to be disenchanted, so we did several dry runs to make certain we were as efficient as possible. The valet parking turnaround took only four minutes. These seemingly unimportant details can make a big difference.

As guests arrived at Barney's, they immediately entered a New York street scene complete with street drummers, voguers from the House of Extravaganza in the store windows, and jugglers who charged the air with electricity. We featured fun street food, a la New York, and inside had the more sophisticated big city cocktails and hors d'oeuvres. As the guests left, they were given small maps to direct them to the next party venue following at the Menil Collection.

Most of the volunteers meet only once and sometimes twice during an event. It's hard to believe that they have the same precision as a well-rehearsed play. I try not to burden them with unnecessary meetings. I always go over the details on the manifesto a few days prior to the event to make certain we are on schedule and to allow for any necessary last-minute changes.

At the Challenger Center Gala, the Urban Animals street skaters were supposed to skate out of doors in front of the Wortham Center. The weather turned rainy, making our original plan impossible. Instead, they skated in the Grand Foyer on the carpet. It worked out better than the original plan. Having worked together on several other events, we were on the same wavelength. This is when you intuitively know what to do in a situation like this.

If you delegate, you must have confidence in the person to whom you are giving responsibility. To maintain the check-and-balance philosophy, you'll need to follow up to make certain that plans are being carried forward. Best intentions sometimes may be sidetracked. If this is the case, you'll have to work twice as hard to get back on schedule.

I remember a pre-party event that was held in the beautiful College of Architecture building that Philip Johnson designed on the University of Houston campus. We were putting on an exhibit of toys that had been created by local architects and artists. This was in conjunction with the Rice Design Alliance's twentieth anniversary benefit called "A Step Back In Time."

Intuition told me to go by and see how the toy installation was going. When I arrived at the building, no one was there except the RDA director, Barbara Cochran. I was stunned. It looked as though someone had just unloaded the exhibits in the middle of the space we were using for the exhibit.

Guests were going to be arriving in a few hours to preview the toys and place early bids. Our goal was to set up the displays to make them look enticing—that is, if we wanted to get bids on these wonderfully unique items. In a rather urgent situation, I literally hailed down some passing students to see if they would give us a hand moving some of the heavy objects, ladders, and lighting. The director and I became instant art installers. The guests arrived later that evening, never knowing of our dilemma.

So you see, you may be called on to do things you have never attempted. This is a part of the fun in fundraising for me and will be for you. Your supporters should always feel as though you have waved a wand and made magic happen effortlessly.

The Chili's volunteer food service people who agreed to work the benefit for neurofibromatosis, "My Heart Belongs To Daddy," had no idea of the extra time that would be involved when they volunteered their services. The food service crews actually had to learn how to carry the five plated trays. The food service at the benefit luncheon was totally different than what they were accustomed to at Chili's.

The Chili's employees were more than willing to attend extra training sessions in their free time. Coordination between the catering department and food managers at the Westin Corporation and at Chili's made things flow smoothly. In order to keep their team spirit high and show our appreciation, two of the mothers of children with NF and I went to one of their Sunday morning meetings at the Westin Galleria. We spoke to them from the heart, which was very motivating for all of us. Every volunteer received one of our commemorative T-shirts underwritten by the law firm Norton & Blair and a certificate of thanks from the Texas Neurofibromatosis Foundation. It is essential to keep the level of enthusiasm upbeat.

Another way to keep your volunteers informed is to provide a layout of the event, so they know just where to go, and include a schedule of times to be there. For example, if they were working on confirming pledges at the telethon, they would be in an off-camera, phone bank location. It is important that they know where to go during a break. Once the event momentum has started, everyone will be so preoccupied with what they are doing that there will not be time to give out information or train anyone. Everyone should know in advance what is expected of them.

After an event is over and everyone has had time to recharge, it is a good idea to have an informal get-together to discuss any problems that might have developed or consider future ideas and suggestions. Questions central to the ways you judge the success of a fundraising campaign are: who was reached, how much money was raised, what is the long-term effect of your campaign, and what is the next step. Keep a folder of the contacts that were used for lighting, special sound requirements, or staging if needed so that next year's chairperson will have a place to begin. You'll be amazed at how easily you will forget from year to year. Put all of this invaluable information on a rolodex or computer disk in a text that helps you associate the contact name and the specific event. You may not use this information for years, but an occasion will arise when it may be helpful. Make this information part of your personal archives.

A media section can list people in print, radio, and television who have been helpful in conveying your message. Under entertainers, I put not only the performing individuals but also a list of friends and high-profile sports personalities like Warren Moon, Carl Lewis, Hakeem Olajuwon, and Mary Lou Retton. Today, athletes have the same razzle-dazzle as entertainment stars.

You will find yourself accumulating so much worthwhile information that you have a fundraising and recycling program and a growing rolodex. You can list contributors by the causes they are more inclined to support. Some may favor political causes, while others want to give their support to arts or medical research. By having an idea of where their interests lie, you will know who to contact and when.

There's no better way to stay organized or prepare yourself for the next event than constantly adding to your personal information files.

CHAPTER 6

The Event

AIDS has been described as a global epidemic, racing around the world with consequences as lethal as the plagues of a thousand years ago. This disease has been all the more devastating in America because it has been viewed by many with indifference, treated as a moral issue and a political one.

The interest and awareness of the American people reached a high when Magic Johnson, one of the greatest NBA players of his time and perhaps the most popular, announced that he had contracted the HIV virus. Magic said he had been exposed through random heterosexual activity.

Today the disease has jumped over the lines. A tainted blood transfusion eventually claimed the life of tennis star Arthur Ashe. In this same way, the wife and unborn son of the actor Paul Michael Glaser were infected, and his young daughter died.

Rock Hudson, Liberace, Perry Ellis, and others from the world of arts and fashion have died of AIDS. So did Terry Dolan, the conservative Republican activist and fundraiser.

Before the end of this decade, experts have predicted AIDS will have taken two million lives in America, both gay and straight men, as well as women and children. Given the intensity of the feelings about AIDS, I felt the need to make a statement. Now I have. Without a context, without the people, all we have left is the problem and the cold mechanics of how to deal with it. My position is a basic one. If you want to make a difference, you don't avoid a cause out of fear or pressure or disapproval.

As an appointee to the Greater Houston AIDS Alliance Board, I was asked to chair the fundraising committee. A vacant historical building, known as the Thomas Street Center, had been designated by the city to serve as the new AIDS outpatient clinic.

Before raising funds or encouraging others to support a cause, I always pay visits to the site and learn about the services and programs available. I feel that before I can ask people to respond to a plea for funds, I need to know just what they are contributing to. For the grand opening event, I used a photograph of the Thomas Street Center on the invitation card to give the site a reality. The Thomas Street Center is not located in the Medical Center and many would not know how to get there, so a detailed map was included on the invitation. I felt we should have a formal opening ceremony before doing a fundraiser. Former mayor Kathryn Whitmire and Harris County Judge Jon Lindsay, who had been involved in making the facility available, as well as other city council members with potential supporters would be part of the opening ceremonies.

Of course, funds were limited. Perhaps nonexistent might be the more accurate assessment. I began to network into the community, and I was fortunate to tap into a group of individuals who were sympathetic to the AIDS cause and wanted to offer help in whatever way. Many of these volunteers were artists, retailers, or persons involved in the design profession. They had lost friends, family members, and loved ones to AIDS.

Because of the opening deadline, we immediately went to work on transforming the Thomas Street Center into a more comfortable environment for patients who would be waiting long hours for treatment and prescriptions.

Amidst our volunteers and other interested people in the community, we initiated an adopt-a-sofa or chair plan so that we could reupholster some of the existing furniture. The walls were given a fresh coat of paint by the volunteers. We put low-maintenance plants throughout which were donated by a local nursery. The Thomas Street staff had their hands full and would only be able to maintain the plants through the kindness of their hearts.

Artists had donated art for the sparse walls. An area was set up for snacks, and a Coke machine was installed with as many other amenities as we could create and offer. I might add, securing the Coke machine was like passing a bill through Congress. Books and magazines were made available. Bus schedules and special taxi information were made known. It was as if a band of magic elves had gone to work moving furniture from the unused floors of the Center to the main floor that was being used for patients.

Many of the nurses and aides had been showing signs of burnout, so sprucing up the Center was a boost for staff as well as patients. On a shoestring combined with faith and hard work, you can move mountains. Just keep telling yourself you can, and you will. The surrounding neighborhood and entrance to the Thomas Street Center were rundown and littered with trash. Even the neighbors became caught up in the refurbishing spirit and did their part to remove trash and improve the neighborhood.

Miraculously, we were ready for the official opening. Staff members were on hand to answer questions about the available AIDS treatment and medicine as our visitors were guided on a tour through the Center. This, in my opinion, was an informative, caring way to solicit support and interest without hosting a benefit.

In order for the Thomas Street Center opening to go smoothly, we set an agenda for the ribbon-cutting ceremony and reception to follow. When you are working with city officials, you must be considerate of their schedules. They like to know just how much total time commitment will be required. There is certain protocol to be considered, such as the order of speakers, when city and county officials are making remarks.

I felt it was a good omen to christen the building. A representative from the clergy, who was a member of the Greater Houston AIDS Alliance Board, blessed the building. All of the balloons, lawn furniture set-up, champagne, and pick-up food was underwritten by a local restauranteur.

What I have found to be helpful in organizing any event is to mentally take myself through the same paces a guest would experience. I try to envision how it works and where improvements are needed. The night before an event, especially if it is in an unusual setting, you might encounter unforeseen elements. You should do a sound and light check if the location dictates. The "Evening of Hope" benefit was held out-of-doors on Jones Plaza. The plaza was surrounded by skyscrapers and street sounds, so we needed to know what the night experience would be and which office buildings were lit at night. We discovered we would need to ask the adjacent building manager to leave on additional lights. With the wind a factor on Jones Plaza, we had to make certain that the tree lights and candles on the tables were secured to avoid any hazards.

We organized food samplings, from beginning courses to dessert courses, from twenty of the city's top restaurants. A detailed map was given to our guests so that they could make their own choice of where to begin on the menu. Port-o-cans for a crowd of 800, including models designed for disabled users, were another detail to be considered as well as how to discreetly camouflage them. Meetings were ongoing throughout the campaign with the city's engineering department regarding supplying electricity to the plaza. The twinkling lights that we originally placed in the trees are still there. I sometimes smile to myself when I see them. I have fond memories of a lone threesome trying to string the trees and call to arms for help.

For the pre-performance reception, which was from 6:30 until 7:30 in the evening, we had to recruit volunteer waiters who would donate their services, as we were really on a shoestring budget. The champagne also was donated, as well as the twin grand pianos for the reception. None of this is impossible. It just involves making proposals and an incredible amount of hard work and concentrated effort. Offering tickets to the event for an in-kind donation is a nice thankyou. The reception following the performance of the play involved the decorations for Jones Plaza, including lighting and flowers. We had to prepare a layout of the plaza for the food service, dancing, and art display. The electrical outlets for the different chefs had to be designated.

The post-performance brunch, promised as an incentive to those who purchased the higher ticket packages, was held at the Lancaster Hotel. This included the corporate sponsors and the $1,000 ticket purchases, which were referred to as the "Heart of Hearts" tickets. The Alley Theater was very helpful in working with us on this postperformance brunch. Not only did Allen Ayckbourne, the playwright of *Henceforward*, attend, but so did the actors George Segal, Charles Nelson Reilly, and Piper Laurie, who was appearing on stage in another play.

Whatever your role in an event, be it chairperson or someone who has been given certain delegated responsibilities, you must follow through until the event ends.

At the reception desk, you can divide the alphabet into two sections. This helps eliminate bottlenecks when all the guests arrive at the same time, and they always do. A seating chart or an easel showing table locations by number will aid people in finding their seating. If you have enough volunteers, they can serve as a welcoming group and direct people to their locations. It gives a warmer, caring message.

As a back-up precaution, it is a good idea to prepare a checklist of materials that should be on hand for the different respective groups in charge. For example, at the registration reception desks there should be writing pens, a cash box with adequate cash surplus for making correct change, charge slips and credit machines, blank checks, raffle tickets which can be purchased, a container for raffle tickets, press kits, and miscellaneous secretarial supplies. If there is a podium, the presentations and speech copies can be stored below on a shelf until needed. If the trophies or awards are too large, you have to assign this responsibility to someone. It will be up to that individual to make certain the items are brought to the podium at the proper time.

The shape of the room should be checked out when selecting a space for an event. It can add or detract from the activities you have planned. While attending a roast of a Houston sports broadcaster, I noticed the room was a long, rectangular shape. This made it very difficult for everyone in the room to have a good view. Part of the entertainment was a lively young group of dancers, who had worked hard to prepare for the fundraising event. Those guests seated in the middle of the room and at the other end could only see the tops of their heads and their legs during high kicks. The dancers should have been positioned in the center of the room or at least elevated on a stage.

Next there was a poignant video at the other end of the room with the honoree talking about the animal shelter and how badly she felt every time she saw a stray animal. This was an important message about why we were there. When you are preparing a video, sometimes the music or mood can bring your audience down. You have to be careful and think it through before you put it before a large audience to make certain you are getting the positive response you are seeking. The touching part is that she had surgery for a malignant brain tumor over a year ago. During her tape, everyone learned just what an effort it was for her to feed her six dogs.

When the roast began, only those seated three rows deep in front of the podium and immediately surrounding the small stage area could enjoy watching Bum Phillips, Jerry Glanville, Dan Pastorini, Mickey Herskowitz, and Joe Garagiola. All of these sports celebrities came to roast and toast her.

Nothing is more annoying than a troublesome microphone that makes funny noises and doesn't work. This can ruin your presentation, the momentum, and the rhythm that is so important. If you have contracted with an audio/sound group, request that they have someone on hand to troubleshoot. And if they leave, make certain everything is working beforehand. You don't want your audience to suffer through your frustrations and your fumbling with the microphone. This also can throw your timing for the rest of the program as well. If you have a guest speaker, not all of them will be as heroic as Neil Bush once was. He simply put the troublesome microphone down and went to the middle of the runway and started talking.

Another detail that is important is the temperature in the room where the event is being held. Most of us have had to watch a speaker perspiring profusely from the lights or be in a room that is filled to capacity so that the combined body heat creates an uncomfortable situation. You don't want to freeze your guests or heat them up to the point where they are uncomfortable. Neither choice is ideal and can detract from the success of your event. Have a troubleshooter talk to someone in engineering who can alter the temperature when this happens. In a way it is similar to looking after a guest in your own home.

When you are hosting a live auction, if an item does not command a bid, always have someone from the staff in the audience place a bid to prevent any embarrassment for the donor, who may be in the audience. If there is no bid, this is somewhat like trying to pull a tooth. When an item is desired, there will be bids. If you force the issue with the audience, you may turn someone off from attending your event the following year. Whoever you have singled out will pretend to be a good sport, but at the same time may secretly fume. Remember, you don't want to badger someone into placing an unwanted bid. Sometimes an auctioneer can set up a comfortable challenge, and this can be effective only if both parties are willing. There are people who like to show off and will only bid in a competitive tug of war where their good deed will receive attention.

If you have door prize tickets that have not been sold by the time of your function, a teen board or members of an auxiliary group to your organization can try to sell them during the reception period before guests are seated. It is a good idea to let guests know when the ticket sales will close.

At an event, if there are unassigned seats, it is gracious to offer seating to your hard-working and dedicated volunteers. Many cannot afford the tickets, and this is a nice thank-you for their efforts.

Two years after the world's worst space tragedy, the Challenger Center Gala event was held to benefit the Challenger Center for Space Science Education. Louis Messina of Pace Concerts used all of his persuasive powers and charm to get the concert stars to commit and donate their time. Because of his belief in the *Challenger* dream and determination, they believed too. That evening Louis had his special friend, Peter Frampton, in the audience, which added extra sparkle to the evening.

The two-hour star-studded show began at 8:00 P.M. and was broadcast live to the viewing audience. Occasionally in an event of this size you will have flare-ups and tantrums, but generally it is someone who has dropped the ball and is trying to cover his or her tracks. Be diplomatic and do your best to smooth the issue. Our star lineup included actress Brooke Shields, Gary Morris and Brandy Brown, both of Broadway's hit *Les Miserables,* country-singing sensation Steve Wariner, Melba Moore, Pia Zadora, and Texas' own hot band, the Fabulous Thunderbirds. There are those frustration matters you have no control over, like Brooke Shields' luggage being lost by the airline, leaving her nothing to wear. You can imagine all the retailers coming to her rescue. Brooke, having just graduated from Princeton University, was the perfect choice to speak on the importance of education.

Much to my regret, my friend, actor Michael York, had to cancel because of another commitment. Melba Moore took over as both performer and co-host, along with ABC Channel 13 anchors Dave Ward and Shara Fryer. The Houston Pops Orchestra provided the backup for our talent.

Our finale featured a 150-member children's choir from five Houston area schools. As the Challenger Project is aimed toward children, the presence of the choir was made even more poignant. The children's choir was organized and conducted by Natt Vaughn, an accomplished musician. Natt is a remarkable individual as she doesn't let her personal handicap of having one arm limit her. The audience was moved when the children's choir dedicated "Flying Free" to the crew of 51-L. As they sang, and at different times throughout the entire broadcast, beautiful space footage was reflected on the screen behind them. A call-in number for the viewing audience was available so that people could contribute to the Challenger Project. Laron Land, a student at the High School for Performing and Visual Arts, performed "Somewhere Over the Rainbow" on his saxophone from the balcony as a tribute to Ron McNair and the entire *Challenger* crew. Ron McNair, the second black astronaut in space, loved music so much that he took his saxophone and music aboard the ill-fated flight on January 28, 1986.

The pre-recorded live messages from the *Challenger* widows and families were very emotional for everyone. This was a labor of love for Jim Masucci, who was program director of Channel 13. He produced two shows, one for the live audience at the Wortham Center and one for the Channel 13 viewing audience. This production ended with everyone on stage singing "God Bless the USA," which has become identified with the Challenger Center. To add razzle-dazzle to the finale, Channel 13's irrepressible commentator, Marvin Zindler, and former Houston Rocket great and member of the Pro Basketball Hall of Fame Calvin Murphy twirled their batons and led the Dickinson High School Marching Band into the hall. As the band marched onto the stage, they played "Stars and Stripes Forever." The audience loved it. The unexpected thrills the heart.

One of my favorite moments of the concert was Gary Morris singing "Wind Beneath My Wings." This was a special song for the crew and their families. While "God Bless America" was playing, the crew for the next shuttle mission, *Discovery,* came up on a riser on stage. This showed our hope for the future and growth of the space program and that the mission does continue. The five astronauts were Rick Hauek, Dick Covey, Mike Lounge, George "Punky" Nelson, and Davis Hilmers. It was very moving, as we all came on stage to join Brandy Brown in singing "God Bless America." Poor

Brandy kept trying to end the song, but the maestro continued playing.

The Rice Design Alliance's 15th Anniversary Gala, "A Step Back In Time," was held on the quadrangle lawn of the Rice University campus. This nonprofit organization's purpose is to stimulate greater public awareness of the urban environment. By sponsoring lectures, seminars and symposia exhibits, the Rice Design Alliance involves the public in issues relating to the design of public spaces, parks, office buildings, retail centers, neighborhoods, and private homes. They serve as an urban conscience.

As guests arrived, they were greeted by a string quartet from the Shepherd School of Music and the spectacular vista of the Academic Court of Lovett Hall. The Urban Animal skaters, attired in turn-of-the-century costumes, glided through the crowd of 450 under the magnificent colonnade. The honoree, the late Dean O. Jack Mitchell, having completed his tenth year as dean of the Rice University School of Architecture, received a specially commissioned "O. Jack-N-The-Box." This exquisite basswood model of the architecture building had O. Jack inside. Fifty-five fanciful toys were created by renowned artists and architects. Well-known artist Larry Bell came in from Taos, New Mexico. He had donated one of his art pieces, *Chairs In Space/ The Game* to the auction.

Guests were summoned to dinner by trumpets. Exotic dancers from a local Moroccan restaurant danced through the crowd and even competed with one another. The patrons enjoyed the sound of musicians Ezra Charles and the Works beneath the balmy breeze and night stars.

For me, it was important that the artists who designed the toys for the auction be included. Artist Gail Siptak fit right into the spirit of the evening with her Medusa serpent hat. Sets of building blocks were constructed by Taft Architects, who had just returned to Houston from being awarded the Rome Prize. Dr. Peter Marzio, director of the Museum of Fine Arts, and Truett Latimer, head of the Museum of Natural Science, were there. Having Julie Allen of the Scarlett Macaw with her collection of exotic birds always pleases the crowd. Her cockatoo, Zsa Zsa, couldn't resist a beaded angel by local interior designer Dale Thwing. Another fabulous dinner catered by Don Strange under the turn-of-the-century vaults complemented the evening.

Maybe once and sometimes twice in a lifetime you have the opportunity to meet a great character like John Henry Faulk. There are many ways to describe John Henry: raconteur, lecturer, folk storyteller, and even a man who performed on *Hee Haw*. His best-selling book, *Fear On Trial,* was made into a television movie starring William Devane and George C. Scott. This dealt with the infamous McCarthy era in our country's history and John Henry's ordeal. He was a humorist in the tradition of Mark Twain and Will Rogers, a political and social satirist, author and columnist, historian, and an astute philosopher. He probably would still be performing if he were here. John Henry was one of those rare men who just was not going to quit.

I have been trying to recall just how he and I collided into each other in 1985. We met while working on a benefit organized by *Texas Monthly* for the Battleship *Texas*. It was love at first sight. He was seventy-three and reminded me of my grandfather, with his wonderful blue eyes, his short stature, and bountiful witticisms. We got along famously from the beginning, and he shared with me a project that he dreamed of doing.

I had been involved before with a regional theater group, and I had the idea that John Henry should have the opportunity to do his one-man show there. We went to visit the founders of the Chocolate Bayou Theater, who just happened to be Faulk fans. We discussed the possibility of John Henry doing his one-man show. I agreed to not only help sell the tickets to the event, but to host the opening night extravaganza.

The opening of his show, "Deep In The Heart," benefited the Chocolate Bayou Theater Company's eighth season. The audiences loved meeting the lovable, foolish, authentic, and outrageous characters who lived in the imaginary town of Pear Orchard, Texas, all portrayed by John Henry. At the theater reception before showtime, a 1941 jukebox evoked nostalgic memories for the guests with vintage western songs. This created the mood for John Henry's down-home humor. They sipped frosty longneck beers and enjoyed a photographic exhibition by two of his great friends, well-known photographers Wendy Watriss and Fred Baldwin, who started Fotofest.

In contrast to the classic Georgian architecture of my home, "Carolina," the country-western celebration honoring John Henry at my home had everything from topiary steers on the front lawn to foot-stomping music by Leon "Pappy" Selph and the Blue Ridge Play-boys. The nationally known Goode Company put on the barbecue. Joe Bowman, one of the last straight-shooters, entertained with his gun, rope and card tricks. Billy George, of the American Hat Company, presented John Henry with a custom western hat to commemo-rate the occasion. Cake artist John Ortega did one of his famous portrait cakes of John Henry in a swirling confectioner's heaven.

It is the privilege of having shared John Henry's vision that in-spires those of us who knew him to have courage to take whatever life puts on our plates.

The rewards of your hard work are realized in the culmination of the event. Don't forget to give yourself the time to reflect on the results and enjoy the afterglow.

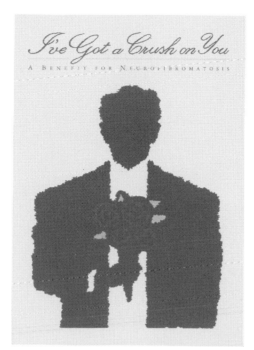

Throughout the "I've Got a Crush on You" campaign, our logo, a silhouetted man holding a bouquet, would reiterate our theme of romance, caring, and nostalgia.

It is important to give your event that spark of originality.

The First Annual Canine Follies, benefiting the Episcopal High School in Houston, was a howling success.

We found "a few good men" to help us with the Children's Museum fundraiser in Washington, D.C.

With myesthenia gravis spokesperson/actor Tony Randall. Fundraising manifests itself in many forms, including galas, concerts, telethons and auctions, to name a few.

Pianist Marshall Maxwell. Utilizing local musicians at your event provides them a chance to reach new audiences while providing quality entertainment at reduced or no cost.

With Houston Ballet principal dancer Ken McCombie. Don't set boundaries on your imagination to come up with a dream for your fundraising effort. Once you establish the concept, you must then bring it to life. (Photo by Jim Caldwell)

The beauty of outdoor advertising in promoting your event is that it is working for you twenty-four hours a day.

Location is everything! For an event like a telethon, high visibility and accessibility are critical. We chose the indoor skating rink of the famed Galleria Shopping Mall for the United Cerebral Palsy Starathon '90 Telethon.

With fashion designer Bill Blass. For "Soiree on the Swanee," benefiting the Houston Ballet Foundation, I noticed Bill Blass was introducing a line of bed linens that reflected our Southern theme. Bill graciously donated the sheets, which were magically altered into overlays for the skirted tables.

Felicia Moon (far left) and Mary Lou Retton (far right). People-watching continues to be one of the favorite pastimes at charity events.

Flexibility is essential in planning any event. Inclement weather forced Urban Animal skaters to "roll" indoors at the Challenger Center Gala, creating even more energy and excitement!

French Consul General Bernard Guillet, Carolyn Farb, artist Linnea Glatt, artist/photographer Frances Thompson, Houston Mayor Kathryn Whitmire, Conoco Oil Company President Constantine Nicandros, and Gilbert Portal, CEO of Elf Exploration, Inc. The ribbon-cutting for "Passage Inacheve" culminated a year-long celebration of freedom, with the festivities peaking on Bastille Day.

Alley Theater

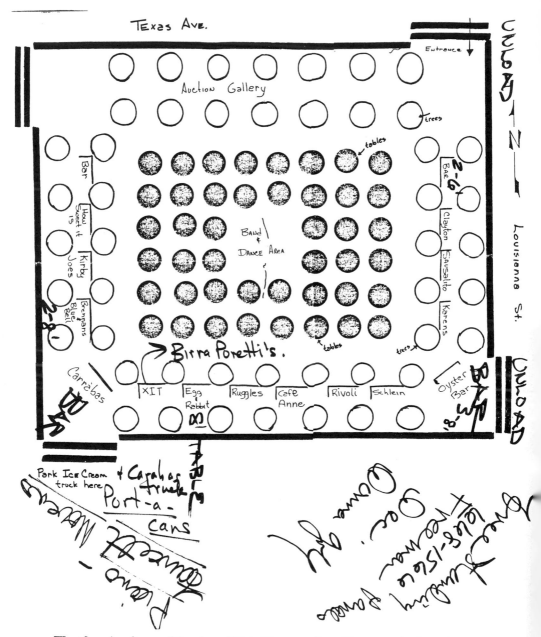

Texas Ave.

Entrance

Auction Gallery

trees

Bar

How Sweet it IS

Kirby Joes

Brenans Blue Bell

Birra Poretti's.

BAND & DANCE AREA

tables

tables

trees

Bar

2-6'

Clayton

Sausalito

Karens

Louisiana St.

Carrabas

XIT | Egg & Rabbit | Ruggles | Cafe Anne | Rivoli | Schlein

Oyster Bar

UNLOAD 2 N

UNLOAD 8'

Pork Ice Cream truck here

Carabas truck

Port-a-Cans

The planning for our "Evening of Hope" party on Jones Plaza required coordinating the rental service and the electrical people with each restaurant donor to determine their needs. A floor plan was essential.

Erin Smith, **Challenger** *widow Jane Smith Wolcott, Carolyn Farb, and actress Brooke Shields. Personalities and celebrities add glamour and lasting memories. (Photo by Alexander's)*

Your supporters should feel as though you have waved a magic wand and it all came together.

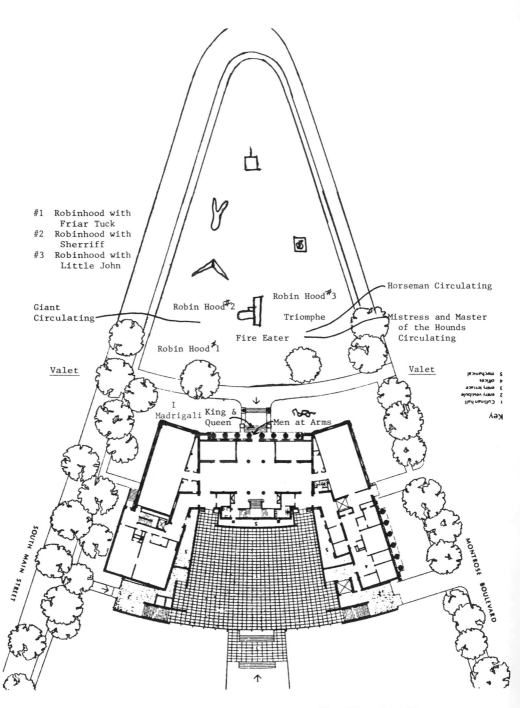

#1 Robinhood with
   Friar Tuck
#2 Robinhood with
   Sherriff
#3 Robinhood with
   Little John

Giant
Circulating

Robin Hood #2

Robin Hood #3

Horseman Circulating

Triomphe

Mistress and Master
of the Hounds
Circulating

Fire Eater

Robin Hood #1

Valet

Valet

Key
1 Cullinan hall
2 entry vestibule
3 entry terrace
4 offices
5 mechanical

I Madrigali

King &
Queen

Men at Arms

SOUTH MAIN STREET

MONTROSE BOULEVARD

One way to keep your volunteers informed is to provide a blueprint of the event so they know just where to go and when.

Former Houston Chronicle *society writer Betty Ewing (background) and actress Cloris Leachman. A touch of showbiz fun was in order as actress Cloris Leachman says hello to an exotic bird from the Scarlett Macaw before the preview performance of Alan Ayckbourn's play* Henceforward *at "Evening of Hope."*

The late journalist-television host John Davenport, Warren Moon, Carolyn Farb. Houston Oiler quarterback Warren Moon actually gave the shirt off his back and donated other personal memorabilia for the Sportsmania auction.

Some people will go to any length for charity. Former Houston radio personality "Moby" raised $15,000 single-handedly by having his hair cut during the pre-party for the United Cerebral Palsy telethon. (Jim Pruett in background.)

'Renaissance Evening' dazzles guests

Your creativity will set your event apart from the multitude of others and make yours a success. (San Antonio Light, *October 5, 1981)*

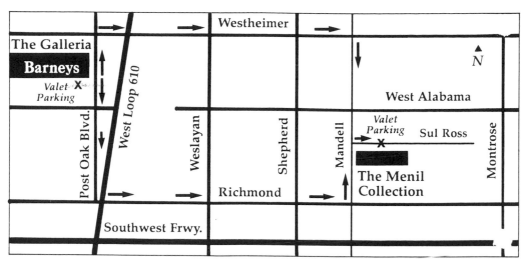

One of the major obstacles for the Change, Inc. benefit was to move guests from one venue to the next as painlessly as possible. An easy-to-follow map was the answer.

Dr. John Stehlin, Carolyn Farb, Ann Margret, Marvin Hamlisch, Liza Minnelli, Alan King, Crystal Gayle. An All-Star line-up of some of the biggest names in entertainment helped make our "Million Dollar Evening" an overwhelming success. (Photo by Beth Beauloc)

To Carolyn Farb, My Angel

Hearts, I promise I wont throw any darts. Lots of people live in a bubble. But you help people who are in trouble. You know you're very nice, when you cook its sugar and spice. I am going bye, bye. And love I can see in both your eyes!

Love,
Nathaleena Smikle

I'll never forget receiving this poem about angels dedicated to me with an accompanying scrapbook of valentines from the gifted and handicapped children at T. H. Rogers School.

Local celebrities and personalities turned out in force to sing the praises of "40 Plus" during the taping of their public service announcement. Included were Councilwoman Eleanor Tinsley, Carolyn Farb, former Houston police chief Lee Brown, Leonel Castillo, basketball star Jim Petersen, and the Antioch Baptist Choir.

Remember to show appreciation to volunteers, supporters, and benefactors who donate their time, energy, and funds. We all want to be appreciated for our efforts, and no one wants to be taken for granted.

Jane Smith Wolcott, singer Melba Moore, Cheryl McNair, and June Scobee Rodgers. Stars from all walks of life entertained at the Challenger Center Concert to help establish learning centers throughout the United States for students interested in the space science program. (Photo by Peter Yenne)

A picture says a thousand words as members of the local business, arts, medical, and social communities join together to show their support for a controversial cause.

CHAPTER 7

Special Touches

Any event is enhanced by special touches of creativity. Giving a little extra thought to decorations, location, food presentation, and entertainment can make a lasting impression.

Decorations are the interpretation of your theme. If done successfully, these decorations will complement the illusion you are creating. The table tops at gala events, with all of their fancied window dressing, are somewhat reminiscent of the many ways you can decorate a Christmas tree.

The tables create a first impression when guests walk into a ballroom, or whatever your setting is. It is like, *Voila!,* pulling a cloth off of some wonderful surprise. That's the excitement you hope to illicit. You will want a centerpiece for your table which allows the eight to ten guests to converse and still see one another. A centerpiece should dominate the space only if it floats high above the table. This means the arrangement should be tested by someone who is above average height.

For the Challenger Center Gala after-party, I decided to use minerals and corals from the Museum of Natural Science Education Collection, with flowers carefully placed and lit by votive candles. Somehow it gave the illusion of moon walking amidst celestial rocks.

When you are working with a city facility, you have to follow certain rules. To begin with, you are required to use the caterer they have under contract. I had to get special permission to provide a lunch that had been donated by a local restauranteur for the celebrities, crews, the children's choir, members of the marching band, and staff. Welcome baskets were placed in each performer's dressing room to appropriately greet them.

Not only did I have to work out the arrangements for the reception in the Grand Foyer of the Wortham Center for 1,200 people, but additionally I had to plan the menu, music, and other party details after the concert. The chef at the Four Seasons Hotel, Robert McGrath, produced a menu titled "A Tribute To American Cuisine."

A layout of the floor plan had to be determined in the foyer at the Wortham Center so that the food service and a view of the musicians would not be obstructed. Our $250 special-ticket purchasers had a private reception in the Founders Salon. A fog machine provided special effects during the reception, and Service America Corporation food service personnel wore flight suits.

Our invitations were coordinated with the space theme and rekindled in our minds man's first walk on the moon. The cover for the invitation and program was a print by Andy Warhol called *Moon Walk*. Ironically, Buzz Aldrin was the astronaut in the print, which we didn't realize until later. This was a total surprise, and Buzz was presented with a print from the Warhol Foundation. Having former astronauts like Commander Aldrin, resplendent in his medals, and Col. Walt Cunningham filled the air with a special glamour that belongs to our space explorers.

A local band, Atwood and Comeaux, played for this final part of the evening, a quality time for the entertainers and special patrons.

While attending a function at the Brown Convention Center, I happened to notice a photographer taking Polaroids of guests. I asked if she would be interested in snapping instant photos of guests and celebrities at a fundraiser for the Challenger Center. Kodak donated the film and the group of photographers their time. It never hurts to ask! Giving guests the opportunity to have their pictures taken with Brooke Shields or Gary Morris and receive an instant autograph as well was a winning combination.

Menu cards and programs give your guests an idea of how the evening will proceed and let them know who has been responsible for the evening they are about to enjoy. Name tags are a helpful idea and add a personal touch in certain situations. They enable people to engage in conversation without having to access their social memory.

If your event is held in a downtown building site, and the parking garage is dreary, consider dressing the main valet attendants in black-tie or in a costume relating to the theme. Oriental or decorative rugs and plants can be placed inside the entrance or near the elevator bank to make the arrival more grand.

When a group like the Allied Florist Association takes on your cause, each centerpiece can be unique and stand on its own or coordinate with an overall theme. In every city there are floral associations, which will lend their support on occasion. As this is their livelihood, the choice is theirs—but, once again, it never hurts to ask.

Favors always provide an element of delight. Whenever possible, they should have a life beyond the event and not be a perfume sample that anyone can pick up in a department store with a purchase. The thought and imagination you put into the gesture of a party favor will be remembered. By doing something that is not anticipated, you will create a lasting impression.

In today's demanding world, where people are called upon constantly for their support, we must not take their generosity for granted. These are the individuals, corporations, or foundations whose names appear on the invitation, who have gone to bat for you. They have exhibited good faith in your cause and in your ability to carry out a fundraising plan by their early financial commitment. The use of their names on the invitation, letterhead, or program is important and encourages others to lend support.

Usually one of the underwriters, especially if it is a retail business, may want the exclusivity and will work with you in securing gifts. It is an unwritten rule that you will not contact a competitor of a major sponsor once you have shaken hands. This is probably one of the few instances where the unspoken word and handshake still work.

Neiman Marcus produced the fashion extravaganza for the neurofibromatosis benefit and underwrote the Baccarat hearts which were given to our benefactors. We decided not to inscribe the Baccarat hearts, as this sometimes takes away from the inherent beauty of the work of art. I dealt directly with the store vice-president, Gayle Dvorak, and their public relations director in selecting these unique gifts. A personal note or letter accompanying the package, expressing just how much their support has meant to the campaign, will be meaningful.

Every guest who attended the Valentine's Day "My Heart Belongs To Daddy" luncheon received a large chocolate heart and a personalized bib for eating the baby back ribs we served. The Runway Heart Throbs received gift certificates for a future lunch at Chili's since they were too busy performing their modeling chores.

With the "Soiree on the Swanee" benefit for the Houston Ballet, one of the very active board members who had an import company came to my rescue. After brainstorming about our Southern theme and trying to come up with unique favors, we decided on black ebony walking sticks with the date of the Ballet Ball inscribed on the cane handle for the men and lace ivory fans with a white silk gardenia and dance card for the ladies.

For the event I secured Mike Carney's orchestra from New York, a favorite with the ballet crowd. I named the rooms surrounding the main ballroom after parishes in Louisiana. In the Lafayette Parish, the Rag Street Rascals entertained, while Bob Murray and the Bayou Banjo Boys filled the air with their sound in the New Orleans Parish. Additional violinists, harpists, and guitarists permeated the other rooms so that everyone was entertained on an equal basis, although they may not have been seated in the main ballroom. The honorary host underwriters for the evening were designated as "Distinguished Citizens of the Beauregard Parish" and were seated in the main ballroom.

I worked with artist Helene Pfeffer in designing a really slick invitation that was shiny black with silver stars. We began a door-prize ticket campaign with a goal of $75,000. A kickoff event for the committee members and captains was hosted by a local restaurant, and a final party was held in my home. The father of one of the door-prize team captains shared his pecan praline recipe from Opelousas, Louisiana. To show our appreciation for his decadent pralines, we created "I'm Nuts About the Houston Ballet" aprons and presented them to him with gratitude. Incentive prizes were awarded to the top team captain and top three workers.

The list of door prizes read like the world's ultimate Christmas gift catalog: a Fred Joaillier 18-karat gold and diamond necklace; a holiday in Southern France for two; a $3,000 gift certificate from Revillon Furs and Saks Fifth Avenue with the message, "You Make Your Own Selection"; a Russian evening for sixteen at the famed Tony's Restaurant Wine Cellar, with authentic gypsy music; a one-week stay in Dallas' luxurious health resort, the Greenhouse, with transportation donated by Neiman Marcus; a thoroughbred filly foal named Sweet Carolyn, great for running, jumping, or pleasure; and His and Her Honda Express mopeds. We placed posters that listed our door prizes in locations throughout the city. Not only did we reach our goal of $75,000 but we exceeded it by $25,000, establishing a record and a precedent.

Your menu needs to be harmonious with your theme. It should always be served hot (if intended to be hot) and with showmanship. Presentation is a large part of food. Reading the food sections in local newspapers or cookbooks can inspire future ideas.

In 1984 the first "Score of Suppers" was held as a fundraiser for the Society for the Performing Arts. The idea came to me while reading an article by James Beard. In his food column he wrote about the "Night of 100 Dinners" to aid the New York Library System.

I thought this would be a unique concept for the Society for the Performing Arts (SPA). Previously, they had held a gala evening following a guest performance by Baryshnikov and the Royal Ballet and another following the Israel Philharmonic Orchestra conducted by Leonard Bernstein. The SPA Angels, an auxiliary group made up of $1,000 contributors, provided a certain amount of the SPA's budget, but there was still the necessity of additional funding. Now was the time to come up with another concept. I hoped we could bring in $40,000 to start.

The basic idea would be to involve 400 people at $100 per person in this new concept, which was different from the usual fundraising format. We had to enlist twenty to thirty hosts/hostesses and ask them to give dinners for ten to thirty guests. The size of the home or restaurant would determine the number of guests for each of the hosts. For example, what baseball fan wouldn't enjoy a dinner with Tommy Lasorda? Having the opportunity to discuss world affairs with Dr. Henry Kissinger might be appealing to another person.

All the dinners could occur in one evening or could be held on two separate weekends. Each dinner reflected the imagination and creativity of the volunteer host. The dinners could range from black-tie, to costume, to casual. They could have a theme, such as Indian, Chinese, Moroccan, celebrity, or mystery guest. The dinner could be held in a variety of settings, ranging from your kitchen to the top of the Transco Tower. A dinner for which patrons pay $100 should be grand enough that they want to come back year after year. The cost incurred by the host and hostess is tax deductible to the extent allowed by the law.

On one occasion, my co-host and well-known caterer, Jackson Hicks, and I created a Russian evening for the Society for Performing Arts annual fundraiser. The food editor at *The Houston Chronicle,* Ann Criswell, liked the idea and had Jackson and me dress Russian for the photograph. She featured the Russian menu as it was going to be presented in a color layout. This sparked interest in the variety of dinners that were being offered that year for the SPA's benefit. Such publicity is another way to inform the public about the upcoming event and get new people involved who may not be on a mailing list.

In the past, in addition to the Russian Evening, at the "Score of Suppers Evening" the themes have been Bro idway musicals and film classics. As a film classic, I selected *Gone With The Wind.* I thought it would be fun to be mistress of Tara. You are guaranteed to have fun doing the research on recreating the Tara theme.

A neighbor of mine, Stewart Morris, is very much the Southern gentleman and a collector of carriages. He offered the use of his horsedrawn Landau carriages and provided us with grooms dressed in full livery. All of the guests came dressed in antebellum finery. We had fun with the Southern menu of jalapeño corn fritters, baked ham with hot sweet mustard, stuffed chicken breast with honey glaze, garlic cheese grits, green beans with almonds, buttermilk chive biscuits, Southern pecan pie, and bread pudding with frangelico sauce.

We wanted to organize a guest list different from the regular SPA mailing list, so we asked supporters, committee members, board members, and friends of the SPA to submit a list of names to receive invitations. This helped expand the SPA's audience. The guests who attended the dinner had the opportunity to meet new friends and share interests in a more intimate setting.

On the response card, we asked for a first, second, and third choice of a dinner they wanted to attend. Where they went to dinner was determined by their early response. Several corporate supporters would buy an entire dinner at someone's home. Others preferred the spontaneity of meeting new people. The "Score of Suppers" was a fresh alternative to the big galas. Guests had the opportunity to get to know one another and move beyond superficial conversations.

To show their appreciation to the dinner hosts, the SPA offered several incentives: a one-year membership in the SPA Angels, listing their name in the program, complimentary front orchestra tickets, the privilege of attending the Green Room receptions at intermission, and the opportunity to meet interesting people in an intimate setting. Most importantly, it was stressed that participation as a host/hostess helped the organization raise the needed operating funds to support the upcoming season's events.

There are foods we all remember from childhood and think are never sophisticated enough to be served at a social engagement. Wrong! You change the order. You'll find people really enjoy eating ribs, chicken fried steak, and cheeseburgers. All of these can be fun and prepared in a gourmet manner if you choose. I have even served chicken fried steak in the chicest of wine cellars.

At a political fundraiser for Houston's former mayor, Kathryn J. Whitmire, I chose a rock and roll theme with a jukebox design for the invitation. The event was called "Rocking and Rolling with Kathy." Vintage cars were parked at the entrance to the party. An authentic rock and roll band wore T-shirts for our candidate. The Pappas family, owners of a local restaurant chain, prepared '50s food.

If your theme dictates Southern, work with the chef and offer treasured family recipes. At the Ballet Ball's "Soiree on the Swanee," offerings included hot cheese puffs, homemade potato chips sprinkled with Parmesan cheese, stuffed mushroom canapes, shrimp creole a la the Old South, and French silk chocolate pie. You might offer Ramos gin fizzes for fun and Southern Comfort later in the evening. The menu card was fashioned after the ladies' fan favors, complete with a white silk gardenia and written with French flourish. It is a good idea to do a food tasting with several of the committee members beforehand so you won't have any surprises.

Just as it was with the Economic Summit Media Party, I knew that the groups of people who would be attending the Change, Inc. benefit would be totally different from one another. So, for the Change, Inc. event we repeated the Cajun theme that had worked well for the Summit. The visiting foreign press had enjoyed the Cajun delights complemented by Zydeco music, and so would the artist, Robert Rauschenberg and the Change, Inc. benefit supporters. It's not every day that one can dine on fried alligator tails, crawfish etoufee, red beans and rice, fried catfish, corn on the cob, and boiled crawfish. (Just for the record, there is a big difference between Cajun and Creole cooking.) When a theme works well and you know your audience will be different, repeat the theme and always add a new ingredient each time. For the Change, Inc. event, the members of the band Beausoleil were personal friends of Bob's. I managed to contact them directly, so it was an additional surprise for our guest of honor.

You can use a private country club ballroom if you find a member for sponsorship. Many private clubs enjoy the additional revenue it takes to keep them going, especially when individuals and corporations are cutting back. A Junior League organization usually can accommodate large luncheon meetings and seminars, in addition to evening functions. Various museums, such as the Museum of Natural Science or the Museum of Fine Arts, or buildings such as Cohen House at Rice University, the University of Houston Architectural School, or downtown bank building lobbies encourage using their space. Of course, they do charge a rental fee. The site you choose is an important part of your decor. It provides the backdrop for the theme you are trying to express.

If you choose a location that is out of the ordinary, you will have a different set of circumstances to consider. Using the skating rink for a telethon or luncheon called for many meetings to work out the floor plan, sound, lighting, how guests or telethon workers entered the rink. As soon as we knew when The Galleria would close the rink, a schedule was planned. We made arrangements for volunteer parking, a ramp for the handicapped, volunteer security, locations for registration tables and seating charts, directionals, and restroom facilities. For the neurofibromatosis benefit, our guests were valet parked behind Neiman Marcus. The lot was closed to regular valet store traffic during the hours of the event. A heart path not only was part of the decor but directed our guests where they needed to go.

The energy level was electric as guests arrived at the "Million Dollar Evening Concert." They were greeted by our bold marquee, klieg lights, and lots of photographers and media. This is the Cecil B. DeMille I speak about that fundraising brings out in all of us.

The renowned, high-stepping Kashmere High School Marching Band was playing in the front of Jones Hall. Celebrities like Vic Damone, Peter Frampton, and Roger Smith were visible in the crowd. A local New York cable network was videotaping the entire event and the pre-activities that led up to the evening. Coincidentally, to build momentum the crew went to the Houston Livestock Show and Rodeo and taped some live interviews about the "Million Dollar Evening" benefiting the Stehlin Foundation for Cancer Research.

Bouquets of flowers were brought onstage as the concert ended. I'll never forget the feeling of being on that stage, seeing it all come to fruition, thanking everyone who had made that great evening possible. When the adrenalin starts pumping, that's what keeps you going—even when you are exhausted. The Jamail family grocers sent lavish baskets of fruit backstage to all the performers.

All of this planning gives your event those special touches. If you treat your stars, your donors and volunteers well, you can call on them again.

Beatrice and Henri Samuel of Fred Joaillier, who had previously hosted a pre-party for the "Soiree on the Swanee" benefit, hosted once again for the "Million Dollar Evening." Involving international jewelers in this way was a concept I introduced, and it has worked well for many nonprofit organizations. The jeweler would generally underwrite part of the event expenses, contribute door prizes, and give a percentage of sales profit to the organization. Jewelers bring a lot of glamour and invite special celebrities to attend these events, which takes people out of the normal routine.

The favors at the "Midnight Supper With The Stars" were unique. I had been contacted by Perugina Chocolates, who wanted to introduce their candies at one of my fundraising events. We came up with an elegant imperial-styled egg of chocolate, each one unique and reminiscent of the beautiful Russian Faberge eggs. The favors were quite a conversation piece and added to the table decor. A fun robot named Gargon was busy trying to cut in on the dance floor.

For one of the pre-events for the "Million Dollar Evening," a ski party and fashion show were held at the local disco called Boccaccio. My friend Suzie Chaffee, one of the world's most famous skiers, was a special guest of honor. She was dressed in a hot pink Wonder Woman-like outfit. The guests dressed in ski clothes, even though the only snow was an anticipated adventure. Suzie had donated a dream vacation at her chalet in Sun Valley. We worked with Continental Airlines, which underwrote all of the air transportation for the stars, Suzie's included.

For the "Evening of Hope," in keeping with the zero budget, local florists united throughout the city and donated the all-white flowers we chose for our theme. The all-white flowers complemented giant silver stars on loan from a design firm that had made them for the Texas Governor's Inaugural Ball. While volunteers were stringing the lights for the trees around Jones Plaza, a couple of street people joined in and helped. They even guarded the plaza while the designers took a break and went home to change into their tuxedos.

Auction items, including more than forty artworks donated by local artists, were on display for final bidding after the play which was part of the event. A committee chair for the art, along with a committee of volunteers, was positioned in the art gallery of the plaza. The volunteers were dispersed between the artworks so that they could assist guests with the bidding and offer any knowledge or information on the artists. A minimum bid and minimum increase were listed on each bid sheet. During the auction period, different artists were recognized from the bandstand. When the bidding was closed, the art committee helped guests with bags or boxes to take home their purchases. If the works were too large for this type of transport, arrangements for delivery were made. Lighting that section had to be done with care so that people could see what they were bidding on. Sometimes I wonder how we accomplished it all.

A luncheon after "A Renaissance Evening" was scheduled in the Masterson Gallery of the Museum of Fine Arts, and, as a special treat, the senior curator of 20th century art, Barbara Rose, lectured. We used a postcard replica of a painting by Matisse called *A Woman In A Purple Coat* from the collection to serve as the invitation. This was a final thank-you for $10,000 hosts, who played such an important part of making "A Renaissance Evening" such a success. When you have written someone asking that they consider becoming an underwriter, or to contribute to a worthwhile cause, it is important to do a follow-up letter. If they accept, let them know how much you appreciate their help and support.

Many of the essential tasks performed to make a fundraiser memorable and successful can benefit from special touches that arise from creativity, strong involvement, and of course, the desire to really please your supporters and enhance your own sense of professional pride and accomplishment. As you will recall from your own experience of attending fundraisers, it's those special touches that you remember—the exceptional creativity, the beauty of the decorations, the unconventional food, the memorable favors, the smooth flow of a beautiful evening, the music inviting you to dance, and the follow-up letter thanking you for your contribution.

CHAPTER 8

Neurofibromatosis: The Heart is a Fast Learner

Probably most of you have never heard of neurofibromatosis. I know that I wasn't familiar with the disease. It took me a while just to learn to pronounce the name.

Some of us thought we had been made aware of this affliction through John Hurt's haunting portrayal of John Merrick, known as "The Elephant Man," in the time of Victorian England. Merrick had been neglected, ill-fed, ill-treated, and exhibited for money like a carnival attraction until a sympathetic doctor became responsible for his care. Despite his disfigured face and form, it developed that Merrick had an intelligent and sensitive mind.

Many medical professionals consider the name a stigma and try to discourage the use of it. But the descriptive nature of the name has led some to adopt "The Elephant Man's Disease" as shorthand for neurofibromatosis. It is, in fact, one of the more severe forms of NF, none of which, I hasten to add, can be taken lightly. Diseases of this kind are not convenient. They are difficult to understand, to observe, even to spell. But the heart learns fast. There is treatment. There is education. And most of all, there is hope and research.

To champion a cause like neurofibromatosis involves educating the public about what it is, how a person gets the disease, and how many people are affected. This begins the education process. You may wonder why you haven't heard before about this condition, because neurofibromatosis is more common than cystic fibrosis or muscular dystrophy combined. It attacks one in five people in the world. The dilemma I posed to myself was, how do I get the word out and at the same time begin raising money for an unknown disease and a desperately needed clinic?

Once I accepted the challenge of this fundraiser, I wanted to find out as much information as a nonprofessional could. One of the ways to learn is to go to the place where patients are treated. I went to M.D. Anderson Hospital in the Texas Medical Center to meet with Dr. Archie Bleyer, head of pediatrics, and his staff. Dr. Bleyer was selected to run the proposed NF clinic and, as soon as the additional funding was available, to hire a nurse who could schedule patients and organize the data.

I learned that NF was genetic, but it could also be caused by a rampant, spontaneous mutant gene. The normally nonmalignant tumors manifest themselves inwardly as well as in an outward fashion on the body. The only treatment at the present time is limited to surgery and chemotherapy. Of course, the more outward tumors are obviously as painful as they are horribly disfiguring.

When you encounter someone with this disease and have had no previous experience with anyone having neurofibromatosis, it is uncomfortable for both you and the patient. The inward tumors are inoperable many times because of their location and more often fatal because of their proximity to the brain. When you look into the beautiful face of our poster child, Megan, it is not apparent that she has this disease. That is why neurofibromatosis is sometimes referred to as the hidden disease. Yet a tumor inside her head rests on her optic nerve. Her parents wait, watch, and pray that this does not change when she reaches puberty. Most NF patients and their families feel as though they are living with a ribbon tied around a time bomb.

I realized I would have to come up with a fundraising concept that would be unique for this little-known disease. There are so many charitable events today that supporters as well as event organizers can easily suffer burnout. I focused on a men's fashion extravaganza and luncheon featuring high-profile, community-minded individuals. They would be known as our Runway Heart Throbs. It would be more fun than using only professional models. The well-known names would broaden our base of public awareness and support.

The event, scheduled for Valentine's Day, was called "My Heart Belongs To Daddy" and would honor three dads.

It simplified circumstances to find one men's retailer to provide the men's clothing for the fashion show production. If we had used several stores within a shopping mall, the situation would have required more overall coordination. Perhaps we would not have achieved the coordinated result we wanted. A retailer will more than likely prefer having exclusivity and not want to share the media exposure. Their commitment to the project becomes more apparent to the public.

I like to organize a game plan describing the various steps necessary to take a campaign to fruition. There should be an initial kickoff event that announces the fundraiser and the date of the event. It is always important to recognize the people who are involved early on, as this will generate interest and build support. Sometimes a new restaurant, and in this case a new caterer, will be looking for a worthwhile cause to help them officially open their business. This is twofold, as NF is helped by being able to host an event at no expense, and the caterer or other new business will reap positive benefits of reaching an audience of potential customers.

Remember, I always operate on my zero-budget philosophy, which should be everyone's goal when raising funds for any nonprofit organization. The caterer will host the event at its new location to acquaint guests with their service, and in turn will generously underwrite the expenses of the kickoff event, which are minimal. For the caterer or restaurant, this would represent the initial expenses they would incur for an opening of their own and would cover food, wine, or champagne and printing invitations. Valet parking, if the parking situation is difficult, would be included as well to make the event even more appealing.

The entertainment for our kickoff event was performed by a group that I had worked with on other events. Since Sundays are generally quiet evenings for performers, James Coleman of the Enchanting Sounds of Shinar hoped a paid booking might result from the exposure he would get. There was a door-prize drawing of artwork by artist Dan Allison, which was another incentive to encourage people to attend. Dan was happy to participate and donate his art.

A minimum contribution of $25 was recommended, which brought in additional revenue for NF. Some people who were unable to attend sent a contribution anyway. This is what I refer to as my "fishing" concept. You put a line out and wait. Sometimes you get a fish and sometimes you don't.

A few local sports celebrities stopped by, which always adds energy. Houston Oiler Ray Childress and his wife, Kara, came by after a game with the San Francisco 49ers. This was quite an effort for an athlete like Ray after a big game, especially when the team lost.

The exotic birds from the Scarlett Macaw piqued crowd interest. My favorite cockatoo, Zsa Zsa, always wears a costume befitting the occasion. People are fascinated by the birds and want to hold them. Many are even inspired to have such birds as pets.

The caterer, Martine Levine Ready Cuisine, had her public relations representative work with the media. Our kickoff event served as her official opening with a crowd of 300 guests. *Houston Health and Fitness* Magazine, local newspapers, and two of the neighborhood monthlies picked up information from our press release, which was done in house by NF Executive Director Bob Hopkins and myself. Photographs of well-known people, local celebrities, and doctors from M.D. Anderson were submitted for consideration. You have to be careful to send a variety of photographs to the different media so that they will feel there is some exclusivity.

As soon as this segment of the campaign was completed, I began the next phase. Letters had to be composed to high-profile personalities in the community, asking them in a clever way to lend their bodies to be our runway models. Initially, I thought sixty would be a good number to enlist, but the response was so overwhelming that we ended up with ninety models. It must have been a good letter. This is important for you to remember when you are composing a letter that is an appeal for your project. People need enough information so that they fully understand what you are asking of them and will respond positively to your cause. The letter should be upbeat, carefully thought out, and interesting at the same time so that it will not be put in File 13.

My idea in using nonprofessional models was that the focus would be on the men, their contributions to the community, their careers, and their accomplishments. The clothes and fashion production provided by Neiman Marcus would be the more subtle focus.

There is a timetable to make certain all the pieces fall into place. When the invitations were mailed in February, our listing of Runway

Heart Throbs and underwriters would give the name recognition needed to give this NF benefit a proper launching. It gives an added boost for people to see names they recognize when they are deciding which worthwhile cause to support—especially when it is a first-time event. Everything has to work in accordance with a plan.

As soon as enough time had elapsed for the models to respond to their letters, the underwriter letters were ready to be mailed. This, at times, is like walking a tightrope. There were several names on the model list which would receive an underwriter letter as well. Corporations and individuals like to show their community support. If a financial or in-kind commitment is made to a cause early on, one of the perks for such contributors is to list their names on the formal invitation and in all other printed promotional material. The mailing can vary in number and is usually between 1,000 and 5,000 invitations. For the NF benefit, we sent out 5,000 invitations.

There will usually be one more pre-event, depending on the chairperson's energy and the time that is available before the actual date of the main event. For example, with the neurofibromatosis benefit, the pre-party event honored the underwriters, in-kind donors, Runway Heart Throbs, and anyone who had made a special effort during the campaign process. The pre-event shows gratitude and expresses thanks to people who have given time, talent, and funds.

A local law firm, Norton & Blair, became involved by underwriting the cost of the commemorative T-shirt for the pre-party event. In return, the firm logo would be included on the T-shirts, which would be given as a thank-you to the supporters at the pre-party. It is appropriate to offer supporters several seats to the event including invitations to any pre-event functions. It is so important to show appreciation and more than just good manners to recognize people for their support and time. This will come back to you in future endeavors.

Having a list of underwriters who represent community and corporate leaders on the formal invitations strengthens the credibility of the cause. When the audience you are trying to reach sees names of underwriters they recognize, it helps them make their decision of whether or not to support that particular cause. People have the right to know who the chairperson is, what their track record has been, and where, specifically, the funding goes. The public doesn't want to support events where the money goes for salaries and administrative costs, but prefers that the funds go directly to the cause. The public appreciates the fact that there is in-kind support by donors, that you use recycled paper, and that you respect the commitment you are asking supporters to make.

Part of the overall campaign responsibility as a chairperson is to present proposals for in-kind support. An example of in-kind support means having the food costs underwritten by a restaurant, like Chili's, Inc. If not, the food cost would come out of the funds raised and less funding would go to your organization. When I chaired the United Cerebral Palsy Telethon, several hundred thousand dollars were in-kind donations that UCP didn't have to sacrifice.

Most nonprofit organizations operate from month to month and are constantly in need of funds. As we approached 1992, we were confronted by a number of cuts in national, state, and local funding. Corporate giving has been curtailed because of the sagging economy. When major corporations reduce employees, it is only natural that they make cuts in other areas as well.

Advertising an event can be costly if in-kind support is not sought. One communications tool I have used effectively is billboards and posters. For the NF benefit, I made a presentation to the Patrick Media Group, who had supported three previous campaigns. One of the billboards Patrick participated with was on Jeffrey Jerome, the celebrated hog that was a mascot for Houston's homeless. The billboard is still making news, even in England, regarding Jerome's plight in being displaced from his home. This is the fun part of the creative and designing process that I love.

For the neurofibromatosis posters and billboards, we used a photograph of Reggie Bibbs and Megan Phillips, a young adult and small child, both victims of NF. Megan has the inward tumors, and Reggie is disfigured even after many reconstructive surgical procedures. It was taking a risk to use Reggie as a billboard subject. However, I believe in the combined appeal of the two images. It proved most effective in getting our message across.

Reggie's is a human interest story that can truly touch an audience. I began making calls to the local papers to see if they would have any interest in doing a profile story on Reggie. An editor at the *Houston Post* said one of the reporters would like to do the story. The paper gave the assignment to Bonnie Ganglehoff. She went to visit Reggie in his home and met his family, neighbors, and former employer. His NF is genetic, and both his mother and sisters have milder forms of the disease.

Reggie hadn't seen his first-grade teacher since he was in her class at Grissom Elementary School. Mrs. Johnnie Howell was reunited with Reggie and his family as a result of the newspaper story. She had often wondered what had happened to this young child who was so disfigured. As a young teacher, she had felt compassion for him and wished there was some way to help him but she didn't know how. She was so moved that not only did she volunteer to become involved with our NF mothers' support group, but she also purchased two new suits for Reggie to wear to our pre-party.

Reggie said that being a part of the NF event has done so much for his self-image, as people are becoming more compassionate and beginning to understand why he looks the way he does. In a way, Reggie has become a cult celebrity. When he was a child, he encountered the cruelty that sometimes comes from ignorance and fear of the unknown. With yet more reconstructive surgery on those facial tumors, if the sacrifice is not too great, hopefully he'll find peace. Reggie is an inspiration to anyone he meets. Not only did Bonnie's article tell his story, but it increased support for the NF clinic and research.

The NF posters were distributed and displayed at Randall's Food Markets, Inc., Chili's, Inc., and The Galleria shopping mall. The goal was to place the posters in areas of heavy pedestrian traffic. At the same time, the first of fifty billboards went on display throughout the city, and we had a billboard unveiling. The unveiling of the billboard can become an event of its own and is another way to heighten public awareness. You should always try to think of ways to involve the public. The purpose of our outdoor advertising was to enhance public awareness and place focus on the upcoming February 14 event.

Both the NF office and Patrick Media Group had prepared press releases, which were hand carried to the newspaper and television assignment desks in hopes that one of them would pick up the story. You never have a guarantee, but there is no harm in putting out the information and making the effort. If you get a response from just one media group, then you have succeeded. Channel 13, our local ABC affiliate, sent their medical reporter, Mary Ellen Conway, to the billboard unveiling. She did an outstanding job in her report focusing on Megan, Reggie, and the doctors from M.D. Anderson Hospital who would run the clinic and treat NF patients.

Reggie had worked at Goodwill Industries, so I had invited his former employer, Steve Lufburrow, and their public affairs director, Sherrie Lowe, to attend the unveiling. The ABC medical reporter went back to Goodwill Industries following the event to interview Reggie at his old job site. Reggie had been unable to work because of some large tumors in his leg. The tumors became very painful when he stood on his feet for long periods. Goodwill encouraged him to come back and work at his own pace. To give you an idea of the problems Reggie faces, one shoe costs $500. Purchasing such a shoe is one of the many ways the Texas Neurofibromatosis Foundation helps people with NF.

At the same time the underwriter letters were mailed, I was working on the copy for both the pre-party and main invitations. So, as you can see, just when you have leaped over one hurdle and accomplished one small goal, the next one is just ahead in the distance. The invitation must have substance to impact an audience in order to get a positive response. There are far too many fundraising events and lots of competition.

The one-on-one meetings began with finding a restaurant that would agree to underwrite the pre-party event for around 200 people. I have to have a particular mind set when I go out on these adventures. If you tell yourself you are working on behalf of an organization you strongly believe in, you can do it. This is my personal mantra. You have to give yourself a pep talk.

A colorful new Cuban restaurant called Babaloo had just opened, so I made an appointment to meet with the owners, a husband and wife team, Dick and Glenna Tanenbaum. Glenna plans the decor of their restaurants and Dick handles the management. I told them about NF, our goals for the clinic, and the upcoming event in February. They said they needed to look at their prior commitments and would let us know. Glenna and Dick ultimately agreed to host the party.

Babaloo had a wonderful house band, under the direction of Hector Guerra, which provided the musical backdrop for the party. The bar area at Babaloo provided the perfect upbeat party atmosphere and, if Texas weather permitted in January, our group could spill over to the outside patio and gardens, which made for a laid-back ambiance. Sometimes things don't go the way you planned, so you have to compromise to make rooms, space, and other situations work. It's part of the challenge.

Being involved with causes, you come to know the people and the families who have the disease. Each one becomes a part of you and motivates you. When they hurt, you hurt for them. Donna Ganster and her son, Andy, both have NF. Andy's NF is more severe than Donna's. Donna worked very diligently on the campaign for "My Heart Belongs To Daddy." She organized other NF mothers and patients into volunteer committees to handle the mailing of invitations, package commemorative souvenir T-shirts, sell door-prize tickets, and place posters around the city. Having someone you trust enough to delegate these important tasks takes a lot of the pressure off a chairperson's shoulders. The spirit of your volunteer involvement and commitment is so motivating and it keeps on going.

At one of the final training sessions for the food service people before our Valentine's Day NF benefit luncheon, two NF mothers who serve as spokespersons and their children and I organized a pep rally. We arranged for certificates to be made out to the food service crew from the Texas Neurofibromatosis Foundation, along with a small gift of a T-shirt showing our heartfelt appreciation.

Another fundraising activity was trying to market the door-prize tickets that offered a $5,000 shopping spree at Neiman Marcus complete with a weekend for two at the Westin Oaks/Galleria complex. I thought it best in our first effort to limit the door prize to a single sought-after item. We had the potential of raising $25,000 to $50,000 on the 20,000 door-prize tickets which were printed. In the invitation mailing, two door-prize tickets were included on the chance that someone not planning to attend would either make a straight contribution or purchase two tickets. The balance of the tickets, which were not included in the invitation, would be given to a volunteer task force to canvas throughout the city.

At the luncheon event, The Galleria shopping mall's teen board was enlisted to sell the remaining door-prize tickets. The winner would be announced at the luncheon following the fashion show.

During any campaign, you must work at broadening public awareness at every opportunity. News feature stories, poster distribution, door-prize tickets, follow-up media from pre-events, and flyers mailed through the M.D. Anderson Hospital public affairs offices were some of the ways I endeavored to bring neurofibromatosis to the forefront. There is no limit to the number of people you can reach, and you must stretch your creativity and imagination to the limit to come up with new ideas. Brainstorming sessions will bear good ideas. You must not keep repeating past formats. Always vary the theme.

Radio talk shows have large listening audiences and are yet another market you will want to enlist for support. Through this form of communication you can sell tickets and garnish contributions as well as educate the public. The radio talk hosts give you a lot of time to discuss your organization, and if they receive information prior to the interview they are well-versed on the subject matter and will do a good job informing the public.

Spend a day listening to the different radio stations in your city and make a list of talk show hosts as well as the on-air television personalities and their programs. Analyze which one might have an interest in your event and be responsive to a call or letter. In a pragmatic manner, figure out when your project needs a boost or has a particular message to get out. Then begin calling the various stations to present your cause.

If you are fortunate and lucky with your timing and their schedules, some will set a date for you to tape or do an on-air interview. KILT Radio talk show host John Downey paid me a great compliment on the air. He said he had been on the air fourteen years, and he was impressed by the fact that I called him myself on behalf of the causes I champion and didn't have a public relations firm call. This hands-on philosophy will make a difference for you.

It is helpful to mail any pertinent information and press clippings on the project to the person you will be talking with. Briefing them in advance will create a more interesting interview and help conversation flow. If possible, invite a spokesperson for the cause from the agency director's office. That person can talk about the disease, art-related project, or other cause, and the chairperson can speak about the event and its purposes and goals.

When you are in the chairperson's role, you should know your subjects well. Your sense of commitment will shine through. Your goal should be for every interview to reach people who didn't have prior knowledge about the disease or cause and motivate them to become involved.

The fittings for our Runway Heart Throb models were scheduled a week before the event. A form requesting information on clothing sizes had been mailed to our high-profile individual personalities in advance of the fitting, in consideration of their personal schedules. Additional questions on the form were designed to give a personal insight into each one's personality and fantasies, which would be the focus when they were on the runway. Many of them probably wondered how they ever let themselves get talked into doing this. In reality, they were great sports and enjoyed the backstage camaraderie. The fact that they were not professional models but professionals of another type made for a great mix. The models ranged from my son, a former governor, sheriff, county judge, football player, attorney, business executive to a cross-section of high-profile, community-minded people. Of course, a few glamorous professional female models, our NF children, and some toys that men enjoy were incorporated into the production of the fashion show.

All of these ingredients created a fun event. The models had one fitting and were briefed by the fashion show coordinator before going out on the runway. Although reluctant at first, our celebrity models realized they would not be judged by their performance. On stage they adopted the attitude of "I'm going to give it my best shot for the cause." Their energy fed off one another, and they constantly checked details to make certain they were perfect.

The important detail work even went as far as selecting the color of table linens to subtly differentiate the levels of financial support. Another detail that was considered was the folding and placement of the napkin. A personalized bib for the enjoyment of those dining on baby back ribs was a special touch, placed at each chair. (Some instructions on how to eat your ribs would be a fun idea in the future, for those not in the know.) Heart-shaped chocolates adorned each place setting commemorating the Valentine's Day holiday. The centerpiece had more romantic notions. It was to be a romantic day in honor of the holiday that focuses on love.

A time schedule had been planned from the moment each guest valet-parked his or her car, followed the heart path leading to the skating rink, checked in at the registration table, bought a door-prize ticket, sipped a glass of wine, and finally sat down to begin the luncheon. The invitation advised the guests to arrive at 11:30 A.M.

Other considerations included the schedule with the food service people. Is the first course pre-set? Is the wine poured? Do we place the basket of rolls on each table? What time is the invocation?

Should the fashion show begin after the invocation is delivered? When do the waiters clear the first course? All of these many details, which guests may not be aware of, are carefully planned and executed. I like surprises, but not in this area. Therefore, we go over each and every detail. Remember, a detail can make or break an event.

In doing this event on the skating rink, which is an out-of-the ordinary setting as compared to a hotel ballroom, there were several important details that had to be thought out. It was a marriage in a way between the Chili's, Inc. people, headed by Steve MacManus, and the special events manager of The Westin Oaks/Galleria, Wayne Glemser. Even the plating and crystal to be used and the warming boxes had to be specially arranged. The normal Chili-size portion of food had to be altered for the different china we were using. Everyone involved in the project wanted to put their best foot forward and be true to the integrity of their own organization.

Invitations should be mailed four to six weeks in advance of a function to allow for prior mail delivery. Seating charts have to be organized once the reservations have been finalized. The door-prize checks which are mailed in have to be deposited and stubs securely stored for the actual date. These were put into a silver bowl prior to the drawing. We had the potential of selling seventy tables with ten guests at each table, and individual tickets could be purchased at the different levels of sponsorship.

My goal is to try to make everyone as happy as possible with the seating. When you are going over the seating, try to place people together who have made this request on the response card. Sometimes when no one on the committee arranging the seating knows an individual, you have to take a chance and hope for the best. Needless to say, seating someone who has purchased an entire table is the easiest. It is almost like insurance to have as many tables committed prior to the invitations being mailed so you are not dependent on waiting for the mail. Never rely on the mail. The invitation never sells out the event. The chairperson and committee members assure the success.

Selling the tickets to an event ultimately will come down to getting on the telephone to make calls and pitches. Whenever you are out, you may encounter someone you hadn't thought of or who wasn't on a mailing list. Most lists become antiquated as soon as the first invitations are mailed. When I would work out at Hank's Gym,

I'd try to network by selling the door-prize tickets and adding to our mailing list. I've sold tickets while taking a breath on the stairmaster. (Fitness centers are places with good people traffic. They have become the new social gathering places.)

When you take on a lesser known cause like NF, essentially you are starting from scratch. First you must educate yourself about the subject, and then you must create a concept and a plan that will give your cause a special appeal. Momentum will build through media announcements and human interest stories on the subject, as well as the involvement of high-profile individuals. Pre-events should be designed to build a base of support, to target different groups that might be interested in participating, and to recognize those already on board. Explore all avenues of communication to inform the public: talk shows, print media, letters of appeal, outdoor advertising. If there is a volunteer support group, get them motivated. Breathe enthusiasm and energy into the volunteer corps so that they will be committed to a successful event. More than likely, their hearts have already made them quick learners.

CHAPTER 9

Swine Before Pearls:
Jerome's Story

Over the years I have given my time, heart, and imagination to a variety of noble causes: raising funds to fight diseases that kill, to endow the arts, and honor American heroes. Without question, the most unusual of these involved a lovable, pink pig named Jeffrey Jerome.

And therein lies a message, a real one: that one person can make a difference.

The story is a far leap from what one thinks of as social cause. Unfortunately, there are no endings here, happy or otherwise, only lessons about compassion, about caring for the neediest amongst us, and understanding that a pet pig can, in fact, become a symbol for a haunting national problem.

Admittedly, Jerome's story is difficult to tell without the delight of a smile. At the bottom of this pigtail of a tale is an unusual and unlikely enchanting friendship between myself, a pig fancier named Victoria, and her pet hog, Jerome.

Victoria Herberta is a bright and articulate person who maintains a sense of humor. She is by choice a handywoman, a house painter, and odd jobber. I can only attest that there is both art and charity in her environment.

Victoria is a robust, earthy woman. Her outlook and her history charmed me. She is wild about pigs, the color purple, soft drink

140

bottles, and the whole state of Arkansas, whose university mascot is the Razorback, and whose football fans wear red plastic hats with hog snouts when they go to the games. Victoria would wear her Razorback hat to the special events we did relating to Jerome and his plight, including a billboard unveiling, a pep rally on the steps at City Hall, and a benefit at a popular disco called Studebakers with a 1950s decor. Wherever we took our message, the hog hat went with her.

She lives in an old and quiet neighborhood with an ethnic mix near downtown Houston. Her purple, three-bedroom house is immaculate. The walls are lined from floor to ceiling with row after row of soft drink bottles and orange soda cans. The assorted pig signage in the front yard announces instantly that you are about to enter a unique place. All of this art has been lovingly created by Victoria.

Her fascination with swine dates back to her childhood, when she recalled seeing a picture of a pig in a book and being enthralled with its shape. And, no, she hasn't eaten pork since 1957.

In the summer of 1987, Victoria acquired a baby pig and named him Jeffrey Jerome after her favorite composer, Jerome Kern.

"I got Jerome and he was such a clown," she said. "He didn't mind wearing costumes and people came to see him. They always knew to bring a couple of canned items for the homeless." She had been waging a one-woman battle on behalf of the homeless long before our city or even the national government would admit there were any. Jerome was her drawing card. She collected canned goods, clothing, and blankets, all items needed by the homeless.

Victoria's house, dubbed Pigdom, was such an outstanding example of true folk art that it had become a tourist attraction. Even the mayor and members of the city council showed it to visitors to give them a true taste of the folk art flavor of the city. Teachers would call to arrange field-day excursions as a special treat for their classes.

Children and adults alike were curious to see Jerome. Many had never seen a pig, certainly not a domestic one. Jerome was pink-skinned with snow-white hair. He had never gone near a mud hole, totally oblivious that he was a hog. He ate whatever Victoria ate — pizzas and combinations of burgers and fries. He adored grapes and peppermint candy.

In the sixteen months Jerome lived with her, he brought in over 10,000 canned good items to feed the homeless in our city. That total doesn't include Victoria's donations. She, on her own, had bought thirty-six sleeping bags, eighty-four pairs of socks, 250 knit caps, and shoes. She would go out under the bridges after midnight to distribute the sleeping bags because she felt that was when you really found the truly homeless. They responded to Victoria's gentle caring and hopefulness.

Many of the homeless don't want to go to shelters. Perhaps they feel they are better able to keep their last shred of dignity and independence by staying on the streets. One woman who stayed underneath a bridge in Houston was in her late twenties when Victoria met her. She wanted to work but had no decent clothes she could wear to apply for a job. One day, Victoria brought her seven changes of clothes, a couple of pairs of shoes, hosiery, lingerie, and other essentials. When she gave her the clothing, tears welled up in the young woman's eyes. She said, "Well, Victoria, you're going to come down here some night and I'm not going to be here."

Victoria was back two weeks later and, true to her word, the girl was gone. She had gotten a job and left a note expressing her thanks. Often, Victoria was asked how she could walk up to these tattered people and not be afraid of this or that. But she shared their trust. Derelicts had slept on her porch, had even curled up with Jerome. Victoria said firmly, "I've never felt threatened in my life. I have peace in my heart and I never think about fear."

Jerome had quickly become an official mascot for the homeless, the helpless, the hungry, and unwanted. When the food pantries were begging for supplies and closing down, her regulars knew there was always food at Victoria's house. She continued her rounds to the back door of the city's supermarkets. She had a regular route, starting out at 7:00 in the morning and returning home at 3:00 in the afternoon, her pickup truck loaded with food. She never minded crawling around in the dumpsters behind the stores. Initially, the stores had day-old products that Victoria could recycle. But not everyone was as concerned as the man she met behind the dumpster at Alan's Lucky Seven Grocery Store. His generosity continued right up to the week Jerome was evicted by the city. At the same time, sadly for so many, the grocery went out of business.

Few can imagine, if indeed they think about it at all, the amount of food supermarkets throw away. One store manager saw Victoria taking packages out of the dumpster, ordered her off the property and threatened to have her arrested. She told him, "Sir, your store has a sign you see when you first walk in, a huge banner that reads, 'FEED THE HUNGRY.' That's what I'm trying to do. I am trying to feed the hungry."

Of course, it isn't always a case of neglect or unfairness. We have become, in part, a country paralyzed by the fear of lawsuits and insurance liability. The stores say they can't give surplus food away because of the health code. If someone gets sick, they can sue the store. Better to let them starve. Victoria called and offered to have an attorney draw up a contract that would release a donating grocery chain from any liability. They replied that her signature didn't mean anything.

Little of what I have written here was known to me, when our paths first crossed. When we met in the winter of 1988 during a Volunteers of America Christmas program, Victoria had just begun the campaign to keep Jerome, a thriving heavyweight once up to 850 pounds, at her home. The city had served papers to have him evicted under a little-known ordinance that applied to swine living within city limits. I was planning a "Ham It Up" party for VOA, a ninety-year-old national service organization devoted to caring for the needy. Admission to the party was a canned ham of a certain weight to help fill the Volunteers of America Christmas food baskets or donations of toys or cash.

I had heard of Jerome and called to invite Victoria to bring him as our official celebrity "Hambassador." (I must confess, puns are a weakness of mine. After all the years of formal invitations that go in and out of my mailbox, an occasional play on words can be a relief.)

Victoria's dilemma represented an attack on the problems of the homeless. Additionally, a second issue was involved that also concerned me: the rights of the individual. There must always be room in this world for the most eccentric among us, for they are often our most creative.

All of which meant that we were destined to link up and go crusading against the mentality that exists wherever bureaucrats wield their authority.

Victoria was organizing a petition to keep Jerome home. The 300 guests who attended our "Ham It Up" party gladly signed their names to the petition, and outside the restaurant we had the empty trailer that Victoria used to transport Jerome to further dramatize the cause. We passed out pink, pig-shaped plastic pins with Jerome's name on them. This became our badge of courage, and his supporters wore those pins for months. It had as much status as some of the trendy designer jewelry around.

My intention was just to add hog magic to the event. I had already planned a contest to choose the "hamsomest" man among the city's television anchor personalities. Jerome, it seemed, had come to us from hog heaven.

After I found out about Victoria's difficulty with the city, I was sympathetic and eager to help. We tried to find a civic group or a company to adopt him as a mascot. The Arnold Zipple Society, a fan club for the pig on the old TV series, *Green Acres,* offered to help.

I presented an idea to Rob Schmerler with the Patrick Media Group, and he agreed to donate a billboard to help our petition. Rob was sympathetic to the homeless issue and just happened to love pigs. We held a public unveiling at our first of several locations, and the message read: "SIGN THE PETITION TO SUPPORK JEROME, THE HOG WHO HELPS HOUSTON'S HOMELESS. CALL 523-HOGS."

The hog hotline message was always very tongue-in-cheek. Victoria simulated the sound of hog grunts, which added a certain spirit to the tape.

The billboard was strategically located in the general area of Victoria's house at an intersection where motorists could view it on their way to and from work. The Patrick Media Group made Jerome and the homeless their holiday project and collected needed items, which they brought to a Blue Christmas party at Pigdom. The song "The Ballad of Jeffrey Jerome" was introduced at this event. I could never have imagined the number of pig fanciers who were out there. We even found a famous quote from Winston Churchill, who said, "A dog will look up to you, a cat will look down on you, but a pig looks you right in the eye and lets you know he is your equal."

I managed to enlist the support of a local radio station, KLOL, and their disc jockey, Dayna Steele, to plea our cause for our first billboard unveiling. The CBS Houston affiliate, Channel 11, got involved. Dan Rather picked up the story on the network news, and the coverage literally spread around the world. Friends of mine woke up in London seeing the homeless story and Jerome's plight on the Cable News Network. A reporter and photographer from "YOU," the Sunday magazine of the *London Daily Mail,* flew to Houston to interview us. The English are very fond of animals, and swine in particular.

But nothing could stop the marauders from Animal Control. Victoria's lawyer talked to the city health officer, Dr. Robert Armstrong, who would not budge. He said flatly that Jerome had to be gone no later than Monday, the day after the Halloween party.

He started calling at 8:00 A.M., and called again nearly every hour thereafter. Victoria and her friends were scrambling, trying to find a compromise or at least a proper home for Jerome. Finally, Dr. Armstrong said that if the pig wasn't off the premises by 4:00 P.M., he would bring out a city trailer and haul him off to the slaughterhouse.

"I think he was vindictive," says Victoria, "because he resented the publicity about this case."

The crew from the television program *Inside Edition* filmed us with Jerome in exile on a farm in Hockley and on the courthouse steps. Victoria had 10,000 signatures on her petition. After the first 1,000, the city council wouldn't accept any more. "All of this," Victoria told the press, "didn't come to light until Carolyn's billboard went up. Then the mayor hurried up and formed a coalition for the homeless of Houston and Harris County."

It would be pleasant to report that this flurry of activity produced results, but it did not. Neither the mayor, Kathy Whitmire, nor the governor of Texas, Bill Clements, would agree to be interviewed.

Here was a cause consistent with my work for Volunteers of America and a chance to offer a voice for the homeless. Jerome was the peg on which we hung our story. Victoria and I did several of the local talk shows, appealing for names for the petition wherever we could enlist public support. National Public Radio came to Houston and interviewed both Victoria and me. It was one of their most popular shows and had tremendous audience response because of the real issue involved.

Justice may or may not be nearsighted, but I have concluded that most politicians are. The elected officials we confronted did not wish to have more attention drawn to the problem of the homeless. They ignored Victoria, whose support base included teachers, lawyers, shopkeepers, art patrons, and a favorable media.

Every resource I could think of was used as part of our effort to rally the media's support to raise the level of awareness concerning the homeless and to help us bring Jerome home. This was one of those times when the media reached a broader audience.

A careful handling was required here. Our position was to bring Jerome home, and we had to be cautious not to allow it to turn into a comedy or a fiasco. Today, you rarely attend a charity event anywhere in the country that doesn't have a pot-bellied pig, whose weight can reach 500 pounds, to auction as the new "in" pet.

No one in the city government would step forward to help. Victoria sent out polite letters, hoping to educate members of the city council about pigs, even suggesting a scientific study. She noted how unusual it was for a pig to have one blue eye and one brown. The blue eye foretold weather changes, turning lighter for sunshine to dark blue for rain. They told her that if they made an exception for Jerome, everyone could have a zoo in their backyard. She offered them a solution, saying, "Look, if someone wants to have a pet pig, a pet goat or a monkey, let the person have one such animal. It has to be a neutered male. Charge them a $500 registration fee for a permit. Who would pay that for an animal if they didn't really want one and intend to take care of it?"

Like most city governments, Houston could use a new source of revenue. Victoria thought this was a way to do it. No one in authority even acknowledged her proposal, but the mayor made a speech saying, "This city needs to be a city of compassion and concern, compassion for our homeless and concern for our younger generation." It made the newspapers.

Victoria would have to give up Jerome, the hog who helped the homeless. An attorney, Denton Ragland, Jr., called and offered to represent her at no charge. The press for the most part did not treat the story as a joke. What you had here was an interesting symbol, a rallying point for a cause that was in immediate need of attention. Every argument that could be made was on the side of preserving this unique relationship. It was hard for me to imagine a city government being so removed from popular opinion that it could ignore the support that had been generated.

Jerome was moved first to one and then a second small farm close to Houston, but the conditions were unfavorable and he responded poorly. Denton Ragland pressed on and succeeded in having the $200 fine that accompanied the citation dismissed.

Covering the story, Beverly Harris reported in *The Houston Chronicle:*

. . . Defending a pig is no assault whatsoever to (Ragland's) dignity because he sees the greater picture, he said. First that Herberta is anxious to obey the law; second, that the ultimate goal is to feed the homeless; and third, that there may be a way to interpret the present law so that Jerome could be declared a mascot who serves his community. How is the University of Houston able to keep a (live) cougar, for instance? Ragland is looking into that . . .

Farb hinted that some City Council members may (yet) be supportive. Perhaps the city ultimately will understand Herberta's viewpoint. These are some truths about destitute people according to her:

- Most of the homeless are quiet and polite.
- Most of them are men in their fifties and sixties who lost their jobs and simply cannot find work.
- Most of them are not wine heads, as the general public is inclined to believe.
- Most of them have a hollow-eyed look, the look of hunger and neglect.

We made one more appeal to the Harris County Commissioners Court, asking that Jerome be provided with a pen at Bear Creek Park, inside the city limits. Victoria was unable to appear due to a problem she has when exposed to certain kinds of fluorescent lighting. Our request was granted, but there was no way Victoria could live near Jerome.

By July of 1989, all of her other options exhausted, along with Victoria herself, she moved Jerome back to the pig farm at San Marcos. She closed her home in Houston and stayed with him two months, taking two five-day breaks.

Jerome slept right outside her door on the concrete porch on a big foam mattress with a fan blowing on it. She built a lower rail to keep the other pigs away. "He can't relate to farm animals," she explained. "All he has ever known are humans. It took me one night to litter-box train him. That's how intelligent they are. Jerome has more feeling in his little bitty stubby tail than most bureaucrats. Doesn't bark at night like a dog or scratch like a cat. He's a big marshmallow!"

She could not stay at the farm indefinitely. Toward the end of 1990, she had been unable to see Jerome for seven months. Each week she shipped him a twenty-pound care parcel containing his favorite foods: raw elbow macaroni, cod liver oil, wheat squares, and other snacks. Still, Jerome lost weight, nearly 200 pounds. After the moves, he lost his hair from shock. He was slowly dying.

This became our story. I believe others will react as I did. They will find it touching and inspiring how one woman helped so many and lost her beloved pet.

My friend still collects bread and sweets for the homeless. My fundraiser for the Volunteers of America exceeded its goals, and I continue to support them. But the system has beaten Victoria down. Without Jerome as her drawing card, there is no crowd. She is quietly proud of the fact that for a significant period of time she made a difference, helping many directly and making others more aware of a shameful, growing national crisis.

Estimates of the number of homeless in this country range as high as a million and a half, although the government insists there were never more then 350,000. For the richest and most advanced nation on earth — we still are, aren't we? — the figure is a scandal. President Reagan did no one a service when he insisted that those who were living on sidewalk grates, under bridges and cardboard tents and newspapers were homeless because they wanted to be.

Now Jerome, who served as a symbol for their cause, is in a sense homeless himself. That doesn't mean one grieves for a pig and not for the people. One can do both. The bottom line is that Jerome will not survive without his mistress. Their separation is more than symbolic. It is sad.

EPILOGUE:

Reflections

Over the last twenty years, fundraising has become a big part of my life and has turned into a real passion. It can be as rewarding as a successful professional career, although it has always remained a voluntary effort for me.

It has been fulfilling for me to be able to help others, to create ideas and implement them, to lay foundations for long-lasting programs and social initiatives. I have served as a role model for many who followed my footsteps, and it has given me great joy to see many of my ideas become widely used standards in the business of fundraising.

Over the years, fundraising has expanded from basic causes to newly identified diseases like AIDS and neurofibromatosis. As the need for support increased, the base of donors had to grow. Corporations became substantially more involved, taking on an important responsibility. Hand in hand with these changes, fundraising became more sophisticated, more demanding, and more competitive.

It is my hope that the ideas offered in this book will help you to meet the demands and the competition you will face in your fundraising. And, as my experiences have shown, while you are helping others you are destined to have a ball!

CAROLYN FARB

Honors and Awards

1984 — Chosen by the Luminare Committee to be Queen Isabella for the XIX Annual Noche de Las Americas Ball benefiting the Institute of Hispanic Culture for scholarships.

1986 — Recipient of Illustrious Modern Award from Wedgewood Society, Chicago, Illinois.

1986 — Associate producer of *Dorothy Hood: The Color of Life*, Public Broadcasting System documentary film project.

June 24, 1987 — Recipient of Volunteers of America's Community Spirit Award for outstanding contributions to the improvement of life in Houston, Texas.

1988 — Recipient of the Sixth All-American Award from Cancer Fighters of Houston.

1990 — Recipient of Service Recognition Award from T. H. Rogers School program's Be An Angel Fund.

June 1990 — Recipient of the Diana Award for Outstanding Community Service for work with the AIDS Foundation, Greater Houston AIDS Alliance, and the Bering Center.

December 7, 1990 — Recipient of Pacesetter Award from Cancer League.

February 1991 — Named to *Houston Chronicle*'s "Best Dressed" list for the second time.

March 1991 — Recognized as a "Woman of Distinction" at the Winter Ball benefiting the National Foundation for Ileitis and Colitis Foundation.

May 7, 1991 — Named YWCA Woman of the Year and honored at the annual luncheon held at River Oaks Country Club.

July 4, 1991 — Named one of the "Freedom Five" by the Houston Freedom Festival for achievements in community service, philanthropy, and public service.

May 8, 1992 — The Carolyn Farb Permanent Endowment Fund to support
Visiting Professorship in Neurofibromatosis at the University of
Texas M.D. Anderson Hospital.

CAROLYN FARB

Fundraising Adventures

1970 – One of the organizers of the first Public Television Auction for KUHT Channel 8, which raised $122,000.

1971-72 – Entertainment chairperson for Alley Gala, Nina Vance Theater.

1973 – Benefit chairperson, Neiman Marcus Coty Fashion Awards, Contemporary Arts Museum.

1973 – Chairperson, Super Sports Night Auction benefiting Public Broadcasting System, KUHT Channel 8, raising $252,264.

1977 – Co-chair, souvenir program for the Jack Benny Memorial Tennis Classic for Juvenile Diabetes, with $100,000 raised.

1979 – Co-founder and participation with Score of Suppers, Society for The Performing Arts Angels, and other fundraising activities amounting to $250,000.

March 28, 1980 – Chairperson, "Soiree on the Swanee," benefiting the Houston Ballet Foundation. A record of $250,000 was raised.

October 2, 1981 – Chairperson and creator of "A Renaissance Evening" benefiting the Museum of Fine Arts. Over $480,000 raised.

October 21, 1982 – Chairperson of the first Archives of American Art Texas Project benefit. Raised in excess of $200,000.

1983 – Chairperson and originator of the "Million Dollar Evening," benefiting the Stehlin Foundation for Cancer Research. Raised over $1 million in a single evening. (First person to raise $1 million in Texas for a single charity.)

1983 – Benefit participant for Scott and White Memorial Hospital, Temple, Texas.

1983 – Chairperson of the world premiere of *Sudden Impact* to benefit the American Paralysis Association. Raised $150,000 for paralysis research.

1983 – Member of Mayor Whitmire's Finance Committee and fundraiser for re-election campaign.

153

1983 — Chairperson and hostess for cocktail reception in honor of the foreign minister of Costa Rica, the Honorable Carlos Jose Gutierrez, to support a newly formed foundation to preserve the principles of democracy. Recipient of the gold Freedom Medal in Costa Rica.

1984 — Chairperson of the Stars of Texas Gala benefiting the Ms. Foundation, a national foundation for women. Raised $100,000.

1984 — Gifts chairperson for the New York City Ballet Boating Party.

1984 — House hostess for the Harris County Medical Society Annual Membership Coffee.

1984 — House chairperson for the Cancer Fighters. Raised $6,300.

1984 — House chairperson for the River Oaks Mothers' March Against Birth Defects.

1984 — Member of Texans for Reagan Committee in Austin.

1984 — Fundraiser for re-election of Senator Charles Percy, chairman Senate Foreign Relations Committee. Raised $100,000 in Houston and $75,000 in Dallas.

1984 — Yuppie and Yumpie Fundraiser for Phil Gramm. Raised $125,000.

1984 — Co-chairperson of fundraiser for campaign of former astronaut Jack Lousma for U.S. Senate, Michigan.

1985 — Padrino Noche de Las Americas Ball, Institute of Hispanic Culture.

1985 — Member of benefit committee for Women Make Movies IV.

1985 — Texas gifts chairperson, USO 45th Anniversary Gala. Raised $1,300,000 (auction raised $400,000 of that amount).

1985 — Creator and chairman of first annual Episcopal High School Canine Follies benefiting scholarship programs. Raised $50,000 the first year, $107,000 the second year, and by 1992 the benefit auction raised $400,000.

1985 — Advisory for Health Care Dimensions benefiting Casa de Ninos Hospice of terminally ill children, honorary chairperson for "Celebration of Toys" champagne tea.

1985 — Mistress of ceremonies with Tony Randall, Myasthenia Gravis Benefit.

1985 — Fundraiser honoring Wendy Gramm for Senator Phil Gramm.

1985 — Committee member for 50th American Presidential Inaugural.

1986 — Gala program chairperson for the Crescent Gala benefiting TACA and the Crescent Endowment for Texas Performing Artists at the John F. Kennedy Center for the Performing Arts. Raised $100,000 (one-sixth of the total $600,000 raised nationwide).

1986 — Presenter of "Neotexanaissance," an orchestral gift to the city of Houston. Raised $50,000.

1986 — Chairperson of Volunteers of America Food Basket Drive, providing food, clothing, and other services to more than 2,000 families during the holiday season. Fed nearly 10,000 people with a budget of $55,000.

1986 – Chairperson and creator essential of the "Ham It Up" Hambassador Event benefiting Volunteers of America. Raised $3,500 for the Toy Fund.

May 1986 – Texas state co-chair for the President's Dinner in Washington, D.C. Of the total $7 million raised, $1.5 million came from Texas.

October 23, 1986 – Benefit chairperson of John Henry Faulk's "Deep In The Heart" one-man show in celebration of the Chocolate Bayou Theater Company's eighth season.

1987 – Participant in Society for the Performing Arts "A Score of Suppers" fundraising benefit, "A Night in the Caribbean."

1987 – Hostess of reception honoring Bobby Short, Celebrate Wortham Week, Society for the Performing Arts.

1987 – Chairperson, anniversary reception, "Theater Under The Stars" gala.

April 11, 1987 – Honorary chairperson, Art League of Houston "Metalmorphosis" benefit honoring Texas Artist of the Year Charles Pebworth.

June 27, 1987 – Participant in the Rice Design Alliance fundraising gala, white-collar boxing match to benefit Cite.

July 1987 – Honorary chairperson of the Business Arts Fund Folies du Ciel.

July 14, 1987 – Chairperson, Bastille Day Ball benefiting the Leonardon Scholarship Fund of L'Alliance Francaise. Raised $90,569.

October 3, 1987 – Chairperson, "An Evening of Hope" benefit performance at the Alley Theater to benefit the Bering Community Service Foundation's programs for people with AIDS. Raised $100,000.

December 1987 – Co-chairperson, Volunteers of America Christmas Food Program. Raised $86,550 and fed 3,000 families.

December 19, 1987 – Chairperson, Volunteers of America Toys for Tots Christmas event. Distributed to 3,200 families.

1988 – Chairperson of the Rice Design Alliance's "A Step Back In Time" 15th Anniversary Gala.

March 31, 1988 – Chairperson of the first Challenger Center benefit concert to benefit the Challenger Learning Centers and Space Science Education. Raised $250,000.

June 29, 30, July 1, 2, 1989 – Participant in the Warren Moon Celebrity Tennis Tournament benefiting the Crescent Moon Foundation.

July 1989 – Board member of the Greater Houston AIDS Alliance and chair of the opening of the Thomas Street Center Clinic. Contributions of $12,500 were made during the opening. The luncheon honoring Dr. Matilda Krim raised $13,845.

July 21, 1989 — Honorary chairperson of the Houston Police Department 8th Bike Relay to benefit the Leukemia Society of America. Raised $101,101.

August 2, 1989 — Chairperson and originator of the first annual "Tribute to Excellence" benefiting the University of Houston Athletic Department scholar athletic programs in the name of philanthropists Mary G. Cullen and Lucile Melcher. Raised $150,000.

January 20 and 21, 1990 — Chairperson, Starathon '90, benefiting United Cerebral Palsy. Raised $650,000 (a 100% increase over the previous year).

April 26, 1990 — Honorary chairperson and mistress of ceremony with Ben Vereen for "Just Say No" Houston Chapter "Roast and Toast" gala honoring Art Patch, chief executive officer of AppleTree. Raised $24,000.

July 1990 — Member of the Host Committee for the 1990 Economic Summit of Industrialized Nations. Venue coordinator at the Menil Collection for the 1990 Economic Summit MediaFest. Creator and underwriter of the "Houston's Hot" commemorative favor.

October 25, 1990 — Chairperson and organizer of the "My Heart Belongs To Daddy" kickoff event for the Texas Neurofibromatosis Foundation. Raised $400,000.

November 5, 1990 — Fundraiser reception, "An Evening with Dr. Henry Kissinger," benefiting GOPAC. Raised $85,000.

November 17, 1990 — Chairperson of the Bill of Rights Committee of the Texas Chapter of the American Committee on the French Revolution sculpture unveiling to commemorate the joint bicentennial of the United States Bill of Rights and the French Declaration of the Rights of Man and of the Citizen.

1991 — Operation Wreath, grant proposals, and Elephant Man affiliated activities benefiting the Texas Neurofibromatosis Foundation have raised $300,000 to date.

February 14, 1991 — Vignette designer to benefit The Hospice at the Texas Medical Center at "Desserts & Designs '91" benefit.

March 1991 — Recipient of award from Volunteers of America for work on behalf of the McGovern Three-Quarter Way House for women. Raised funds for a grant of $40,000 over three years from the John P. McGovern Foundation.

March 1991 — Opened Carolina Gardens to benefit River Oaks Garden Club to 16,000 guests for the 56th Annual River Oaks Garden Club

Azalea Trail.

September 26, 1991 — Chairperson, Barney's New York Opening/ Rauschenberg Exhibition to benefit Change, Inc. Raised $47,760.

October 9, 1991 — Keynote speaker for the National Public Relations Society of America, Houston Chapter, and Federation of Houston Professional Women on fundraising.

November 3, 1991 — Chairperson of political fundraiser for re-election of Mayor Kathryn Whitmire.

May 8, 1992 — Chairperson and creator of "I've Got A Crush On You" Texas Neurofibromatosis Foundation benefit. Raised $300,000.

1992 — Fundraising segment of *Lifestyles of the Rich and Famous* on national television.

1992 — Silver Tea for Holly Hall Retirement. All-time attendance record of 1,400 people as well as record funds collected, in the amount of $22,311.

October 1992 — Honorary chairperson of the Emerald Circle, a giving club of the San Jacinto Girl Scout Council Chairing campaign for Sailing Camp Casa Mare. Served as special funding projects coordinator. To date $20,000 has been raised.

March 29, 1993 — Price Waterhouse "Night of Stars" benefit for the High School for the Performing and Visual Arts. Raised $64,450.

April 27, 1993 — Hosted the Friends of the Ronald McDonald House Spring Coffee, with 216 new members and a record turnout raising $9,000.

Due to the many and varied organizations I have worked with over the years, it would be difficult to include them all by name. My contribution may have been large or small; however, the fundraising momentum continues after the initial fundraising activity.

Index

A

A. D. Players, 84
Aaron, Hank, 64, 65
Access Cable Network, 84
Adlakha, Dr. Rameesh, 44
AIDS fundraising, 23, 25, 38–39,
    56, 57, 68, 78, 84, 87–88,
    106–109
Alan's Lucky Seven Grocery Store,
    142
Albee, Edward, 74
Aldrin, Buzz, 118
Alfred C. Glassell Jr., School of
    Art, 81
Allen, Julie, 114
Alley Theater, 19, 23, 25, 56, 68–
    69, 74, 78, 88, 93, 94, 109
Allied Florist Association, 119
Allison, Dan, 90, 129
Amatangelo, Kathleen, 97
American Airlines, 62, 64
American Film Institute, 74
American Film and Video Festival,
    76
American Hat Company, 116
American Paralysis Association,
    46–47
Arbeid, Murray, 48
Archives of American Art, 35
Armstrong, Dr. Robert, 145
Arnold Zipple Society, 144
Art League of Houston, 90

Ashe, Arthur, 106
Astro Fantasy Camp, 64
Atwood and Comeaux, 64, 118
Austrian National Tourist Office,
    62
Autry, Gene, 9
A Woman In A Purple Coat, 126
Ayckbourne, Allen, 109

B

Babaloo, 134
Badner, Andrea, 90
Baldwin, Fred, 115
"Ballad of Jeffrey Jerome, The,"
    144
Ballet Russe, 35, 61
Balph, Larry, 84–85
Bardot, Brigitte, 60
Barney's New York, 53–54, 102
Baryshnikov, 121
Bass, Nancy Lee, 50
    Perry, 50
Bastille Day Ball, 44, 82
Battleship *Texas,* 115
Bauer, Jim, 21
Bayou Banjo Boys, 120
Bayou Bend, 59
Beal, Dorothy, 11
"Be An Angel" program, 41–42
Bear Creek Park, 147
Beard, James, 121
Beatty, Warren, 53
Beausoleil, 54, 124

Bell, Larry, 114
Benton, Thomas Hart, 35
Bentsen, Lloyd, 43
Bering Community Service
    Foundation, 39, 56, 68
Bering United Methodist Church,
    38, 39, 78, 93
Bernabe, Henri, 83
Bernstein, Leonard, 121
Bertha's, 78
Bess, Forest, 35
Beverly Hills, 7
Beverly Wilshire Hotel, 9
Bibbs, Reggie, 84–85, 132–134
Big Rockin' Dopsey and the
    Twisters, 90
Billings, Josh, 70
Bill of Rights Committee, 82, 84
"Black Tie and Boots" Gala, 43
Blaffer, Jane, 51
Blaffer Gallery, 82
Blass, Bill, 25, 49
Bleyer, Dr. Archie, 128
Bloomingdale, Betsy, 50
Blue Ridge Playboys, 116
Bob Hardwick Orchestra, 36
Boccaccio, 125
Boehm, Helen, 48, 50
Boudreaux, Bob, 42
Boutin, Claude, 44
Bowman, Joe, 116
Boynton, Jack, 25, 90, 94
Bradshaw, Bill, 41
"Breakfast in Bed," 88–90
Brennan's Restaurant, 78, 86
Britt, Mai, 6
Broadnax, Geary, 29
Brown, Alice, 34, 68
    Brandy, 63, 112, 113
    Christy, 62
    Peter H., 51
    Rita Mae, 74
Brown Convention Center, 118

Brown Derby, 9
Brown Foundation, 35
Brozek, Miroslave, 60
Buggy Beauties, 17
Bush, George, 16, 18
    Mrs. George, 16
    Neil, 111
Business Arts Fund, 19

C

Caballe, Montseurat, 29
Cable News Network, 144
Cadillac Bar, 40
Caesar's Palace, 7, 10
Cafe Express, 64
"Canine Follies," 69–72
Cannon, Dyan, 6
Carnegie, Andrew, 13
Carney, Mike, 120
"Carolyn Farb Day," 42
Carrabbas, 64
Cassatt, Mary, 35
Chaffee, Suzie, 125
Chairs In Space/The Game, 114
Challenger Center benefit, 15–16,
    18, 31, 33–34, 44, 67, 101,
    103, 112–114, 117–118
Challenger Learning Center, 55,
    112
Chaney, Don, 18
Change, Inc., 53–54, 123–124
Channel 11, 65, 144
Channel 13, 29, 42, 44, 63, 71,
    112, 113, 133
Channel 8, 21–22, 74
Channel 8 Auction Super Sports
    Night, 22
Charisse, Cyd, 9
Charity Players, 41
Charron, Paul, 45
Cher, 97
Cherry, Emma Richardson, 90
Children's Fund, 41
Childress, Kara, 130

Ray, 54, 64, 130
Chili's, Inc., 26, 61, 104, 120, 132, 133, 138
Chocolate Bayou Theater, 115
Christmas Food Basket program, 39–40
Churchill, Winston, 144
Circle T Ranch, 50
Cisneros, Henry, 43
Clements, Bill, 50, 145
    Rita, 50
Cobb, Arnett, 51
Cochran, Barbara, 103
Cohen House, 124
Cohn, Harry, 8
Colaco, Tina, 41–42
Colby, Carl, 75
Coleman, Dabney, 43
    James, 129
Collins, Rebecca, 34
Columbia Pictures, 8
Concerts Royaux, 36
Conoco, Inc., 84
Contemporary Arts Museum, 19, 35
Continental Airlines, 75, 125
Conway, Mary Ellen, 133
Cooley, Dr. Denton, 10
Copacabana, 6
Corcoran Gallery, 76
Cornell Media, 77
Cougar Dolls, 17, 58
Covey, Dick, 113
Cox, Ed, 50
Crescent Art Gallery, 50
Crescent Gala, 49–51
Crispin, Andre, 44
Criswell, Ann, 122
Crow, Trammel, 50
Cullen, Mary G., 17
    Mrs. Roy, 18
Cullinan, Nina, 12, 34–36
Cullinan Hall, 36

Cunningham, Walt, 48, 118

D
Dallas Museum of Art, 50, 51
Damone, Vic, 124
Davalos, Rudy, 16, 58
Dave and Buster's, 24
Davis, Sammy, Jr., 6
"Deep in The Heart," 38, 115
Dempster, Nigel, 50
Desserts and Designs '91, 88
Devane, William, 115
Dickinson High School Marching Band, 113
Dolan, Terry, 106
Domain Privee, 3
Domingo, Placido, 81
Donahue, Phil, 43
Dorothy Hood: The Color of Life, 74–76
Dorsey, Tommy, 48
Douty, Dorothy, 50
Downey, John, 136
Dumont, Gerard, 82
Durocher, Leo, 22
Dvorak, Gayle, 119

E
Eastwood, Clint, 47
Economic Summit Host Committee, 102
Economic Summit Media Party, 123
Elephant Man, The, 84
Elkins, Judge James, 3, 4
Ellis, Perry, 106
El Mirador, 9
El Rancho Vegas, 6
Enchanting Sounds of Shinar, 129
English, Paul, 51, 52
Entratter, Jack, 6
Episcopal High School Parents Association, 69
Escaron, Pierre, 45

"Evening of Hope," 23, 25, 33, 39, 56, 68, 78, 87, 93, 108–109, 125
Ezra Charles and the Works, 114

F
Fabulous Thunderbirds, 16, 112
Farb, Harold, 29
Farenthold, Sissy, 43
Faulk, John Henry, 38–39, 45, 115–116
Female Line, The, 74
Ferber, Edna, 3
Ferrara, Anthony, 90
First City National Bank, 4
Fitzgerald, Frances, 74
Flamingo, 6
Foley's, 26
Folie du Ciel "Sky Follies," 19
Ford Motor Company, 41
Fotofest, 115
Four Seasons Hotel, 34, 72, 118
Frampton, Peter, 112, 124
Frankel, Terrie, 59
Frankel's Costume Co., Inc., 19
Freedman, Jakie, 2–11
    Robert, 7
    Sadie, 7, 10
Fremont Hotel, 6
French Declaration of the Rights of Man and of the Citizen, 82
Frontier Hotel, 7
Fryer, Shara, 71, 112

G
Galanos, James, 25–26, 36, 63
Galleria, The, 19, 26, 47, 53, 61, 66, 89, 102, 124, 133, 135
Ganglehoff, Bonnie, 132
Ganster, Andy, 135
    Donna, 135
Garagiola, Joe, 111
Gayle, Crystal, 16, 72
George, Billy, 116

Giraud, Pam, 88
Gladys Knight and the Pipps, 51
Glanville, Jerry, 111
Glaser, Paul Michael, 106
Glatt, Linnea, 82, 83
Glemser, Wayne, 138
Goode, Jim, 71
Goode Company, 116
Good Morning, Houston, 53
Goodwill Industries, 134
Goodyear Blimp, 19
Governor's Honor Guard, 36
Grable, Betty, 6
Grant, Cary, 6
Greater Houston AIDS Alliance Board, 107, 108
Green Acres, 144
Greenhouse, 121
Greenspun, Hank, 5
Griffin, Jan, 98
Grissom Elementary School, 133
Guardian Angels, 69
Guerra, Hector, 134
Guillett, Bernard, 84

H
Halley's Worlds Diptych 1985, 76
"Ham It Up" fundraiser, 40, 143–144
Hamlisch, Marvin, 16, 43, 72, 73
Hamm, Madeline McDermott, 59
Hank's Gym, 138
Hard Rock Cafe, 49
Harris, Beverly, 146
Harris County Commissioners Court, 147
Harris County Heritage Society, 19
Harris County Medical Auxiliary, 54, 98
Hart, Jerry, 64
Hauek, Rick, 113
Health Adventure, 55
Heisman Trophy, 18

Hemus, Solly, 22
Henceforward, 68, 109
Henie, Sonja, 11
Herberta, Victoria, 140–148
Herskowitz, Mickey, 111
Hicks, Jackson, 122
High School for Performing and
    Visual Arts, 81, 83, 101, 113
Hilmers, Davis, 113
Hobby, Bill, 43
    Diana, 43
Hofheinz, Judge Roy, 60
Hofheinz Pavilion, 17
Hogg, Ima, 59
Holly Hall Retirement Center, 54
homeless fundraising, 132, 140–
    148
Honda Express, 121
Hood, Dorothy, 35, 74–76
Hope, Bob, 48
Hopkins, Bob, 98, 130
Hopps, Walter, 54
Horseshoe Casino, 7
Horseshoe Hotel, 6
House of Extravaganza, 102
Houston, Kenny, 22
Houston Astros, 64
Houston Ballet, 35, 38, 120
Houston Ballet Foundation, 25,
    34, 37–38
Houston Buffs, 22
Houston Business Journal, 88
Houston Chronicle, 59, 122, 146
Houston City Council, 83, 107,
    141, 145, 146
Houston Health and Fitness, 89, 130
Houston Independent School
    District, 45, 55
Houston Jaycees, 81
Houston Lighting and Power, 43
Houston Livestock Show and
    Rodeo, 125
Houston Oilers, 54, 64

Houston Police Department, 27–
    28
Houston Polo Team, 19
Houston Pops Orchestra, 16, 112
Houston Post, 53, 132
Houston Public Television
    Auction, 21–22
Houston Rockets, 16, 17, 18, 64
Houston Sesquicentennial
    Committee, 51
"Houston's Hot," 102
Houston Symphony Orchestra, 72
Howell, Mrs. Johnnie, 133
How Sweet It Is, 78
Hudson, Rock, 106
Hughes, Howard, 6, 9, 10
Hunan's, 64
Hunt, Bunker, 50
    Caroline, 49
Hurt, John, 127
Hyatt Regency, 63, 100
Hyatt Regency Waikiki, 64
Hyundai of America, 26, 66

I
Independence, 48
Inside Edition, 145
Interview Magazine, 44
Israel Philharmonic Orchestra, 121
"I've Got A Crush On You," 24,
    58, 96

J
Jack Benny Memorial Tennis
    Classic, 47
Jack's Restaurant, 63
Jamail and Sons, 60, 125
James, Harry, 6
James Madison First Amendment
    Award, 45
Jefferson, Thomas, 45
Jeffrey Jerome, 132, 140–148
Jensen, Sandra, 36
Joaillier, Fred, 120, 125

Johnson, Lyndon B., 30
  Magic, 106
  Philip, 50, 103
Jones Hall, 16, 124
Jones Plaza, 23, 69, 78, 108, 126
Jong, Erica, 74
Junior League, 124
Juvenile Diabetes Foundation, 47

K

Karoli, Bela, 64
Kashmere High School Marching
    Band, 124
Katelman, Beldon, 6
Katzman, Dr. Lu, 72
Kennedy Center, 50, 58
Kern, Jerome, 141
Kerrville, Texas, 97
KILT Radio, 136
King, Alan, 16, 72
Kissinger, Henry, 121
Kleberg Foundation, 35
Klein, Calvin, 87
Kline, Franz, 75
KLOL Radio, 144
Knight, Shirley, 74
Krim, Dr. Matilda, 84
Krispen, 89
KUHT Public Television, 21–22,
    74

L

L'Alliance Francaise, 44–46
Lancaster Hotel, 109
Land, Laron, 113
Lanz Originals, 9
Lasorda, Tommy, 121
Last Flapper, The, 25, 94
Las Vegas, Nevada, 4–7
Las Vegas Sun, 5
Latimer, Truett, 114
Lauren, Ralph, 89
Laurie, Piper, 25, 94, 109
Lawson, Melanie, 29

William, 29
Leach, Robin, 50
Leachman, Cloris, 73
Leadership Houston, 42
Lear, Frances, 74
Leiber, Judith, 48
Leonardon Scholarship Fund, 45
Les Miserables, 63
Leukemia Society, 27–28
Lewis, Carl, 16, 18, 54, 63, 64, 105
    Guy, 18
Liberace, 106
Lifestyles of the Rich and Famous, 50
Lindsay, Jon, 107
Loews Anatole Hotel, 48
London Daily Mail, 144
Lott, Jesse, 53
Louis, Joe, 1, 10
Lounge, Mike, 113
Love, Jim, 90
Lovett Hall, 30
Lowe, Sherrie, 134
Lufburrow, Steve, 134

M

M.D. Anderson Cancer Center, 98
M.D. Anderson Hospital, 128,
    130, 135
McCarthy, Glenn, 3
McFadden, Mary, 49
McGrath, Robert, 118
McHugh, Jimmy, 6
Mack, Ted, 6
MacManus, Steve, 138
McNair, Ron, 113
Madison, James, 45
Madonna, 53
March of Dimes, 54
Marcus, Lawrence, 22
Margret, Ann, 16, 72
Marigny, Count Alfred de, 60
    Countess, 60
Martin, Tony, 9

Martine Levine Ready Cuisine, 130
Marzio, Peter, 114
Masterson, Carroll, 34
Masterson Gallery, 126
Masucci, Jim, 113
Mathis, Johnny, 6
Matisse, 126
Maxwell, Louise, 8
Mayo, Marti, 82
Mecom, John, Sr., 3
Melcher, Lucile, 17
    Mrs. Leroy, 18
Menil, Dominique de, 34, 52–54
Menil Collection, 52–54, 102, 103
Merrick, John, 127
Merrill, Dina, 47
Messina, Louis, 112
Metalmorphosis, 90
MFA Today, 86
MGM Studios, 8
"Midnight Supper with the Stars," 34, 125
Mies van der Rohe Cullinan Wing, 36
Milieux, 89
Miller, Glenn, 48
    Norm, 64
    Philip, 36
Miller Brewing, 64
"Million Dollar Evening," 38, 124–125
Minnelli, Liza, 16, 36, 72
"Mission Continues, The," 31
Mitchell, O. Jack, 24, 114
Modern Museum of Art, 74
Mones, Manny, 62
Montgomery, Mayes, and Stritch, 36
Moon, Warren, 54, 64, 65, 105
Moon Walk, 118
Moore, Melba, 16, 112
Morris, Gary, 16, 112, 113, 118

Stewart, 122
Mosbacher, Robert, 22
Mottehedeh, 48, 58–59
Mount Vernon, 48
Moyers Champagne, 83
Mrs. Fields Cookie Shop, 23
Ms. Foundation for Women, 42–44
Municipal Arts Commission, 35, 82
Murphy, Calvin, 113
Murray, Bob, 120
Museum of Fine Arts, Houston, 19, 29–30, 35–36, 58, 59, 68, 76, 86, 114, 124, 126
Museum of Fine Arts Gala, 86
Museum of Natural Science, 15, 31, 114, 124
Museum of Natural Science Education Collection, 117
"My Heart Belongs To Daddy," 84, 104, 120, 129–139, 135
My Left Foot, 62

N
Nabors, Jim, 36, 50
Nantz, Jim, 18
NASA, 19
National Gallery, 74
National Public Radio, 145
Neiman Marcus, 18, 22, 31, 36, 119, 121, 124, 130, 135
Nelson, Don, 53
    George "Punky," 113
"Neotexanaissance," 51–52
Netting, Tom, 100
neurofibromatosis fundraising, 24, 29, 58, 84, 97–99, 104, 119, 124, 127–139
New Harmony, 51
New Music America Festival of Houston, 51
New York Library System, 121
Ney, Elisabet, 35

Nicandros, Dino, 84
Nielson, Gifford, 65
"Night of 100 Dinners," 121
Norton & Blair, 18, 104, 131
Nutcracker Market, 34

O
Oddo, Tom, 96
Olajuwon, Hakeem, 16, 18, 64,
    105
"Operation Care and Share," 40
Operation Wreath, 99
Ortega, John, 116

P
Pace Concerts, 44, 112
Pappas family, 123
Parkinson, Norman, 67
Parsons, Louella, 6
Paschen, Henry, Jr., 61
"Passage Inacheve," 83–84
Pasternak, Joe, 8
Pastorini, Dan, 64, 111
Patrick Media Group, 87, 96–97,
    132, 133, 144
Pavilion, The, 64, 66
Paw Print Preview, 71
Peabody, Mrs. Malcolm, 74
    Pam, 74–76
Pebworth, Charles, 90
Performing Arts, 78
Perot, Margo, 50
    Ross, 50
Perugina Chocolates, 125
Petrie, Natalie, 4
Petrus, Leon "Pete," 29
Pfeffer, Helene, 120
Phillips, Bum, 111
    Irving, 51
    Megan, 128, 132
President and First Lady Health
    and Racquetball Clubs, 64
Presidential Yacht Charter, Inc.,
    48

Pro Bowl, 64, 65
Project Coffee, 54
Public Relations Society of Amer-
    ica, Houston Chapter, 42
Putski, Ivan, 22

Q
Quality Beverage, 64
"Quarterback Corner," 65
Quinn, Anthony, 81

R
Ragland, Denton, Jr., 146–147
Rag Street Rascals, 120
Ralston Purina, 70
Randall's Food Markets, Inc., 40,
    133
Rather, Dan, 144
Rauschenberg, Robert, 52–54,
    102, 123–124
Reagan, Ronald, 148
Reagan–Bush inauguration, 58
Reilly, Charles Nelson, 109
"Renaissance Evening," 19, 29–30,
    58–61, 67, 86, 126
Retton, Mary Lou, 18, 64, 105
Reves, Wendy, 51
Revillon Furs, 120
Rhode Island School of Design, 76
Rice Architectural School, 24
Rice Design Alliance, 23–24, 30,
    31, 103, 114
Rice University, 30, 124
Rice University School of Archi-
    tecture, 114
Richards, Ann, 43
Ride, Sally, 43
Ritz–Carlton Hotel, 71
River Oaks Country Club, 58
Rockefeller, John D., 12–13
"Rocking and Rolling with Kathy,"
    123
Rose, Barbara, 126
Royal Ballet, 121

Runway Heart Throbs, 29, 120, 128–129, 130–131, 136–137
Ryan, Nolan, 63
  Ray, 9

S
St. Joseph's Hospital, 72, 73
Sakowitz, 71
Saks Fifth Avenue, 29, 120
Sam's, 40
Samuel, Beatrice, 125
  Henri, 125
Sands Hotel, The, 3, 5–6, 9
San Jacinto Girl Scout Council, 42
Scarlett Macaw, 114, 130
Schella, John, 22
Schiwetz, Buck, 59
Schlumberger, 45
Schmerler, Rob, 144
Schole, Wilhelm, 54
Scobee, June, 15, 34, 44
"Score of Suppers," 121, 122–123
Scott, George C., 115
Security Control Systems, 43
Segal, George, 109
Selph, Leon "Pappy," 116
Service America Corporation, 118
Sfuzzi's, 64
Shank, Bud, 51
"Share Toys With Our Children For Christmas" party, 40
Sharp, Isadore, 72
Shepherd School Bell Choir, 101
Shepherd School of Music at Rice University, 31, 101, 114
Shields, Brooke, 16, 112, 118
Shulman, Kenyon, 69, 71
Sinatra, Frank, 6
Siptak, Gail, 114
"Six Hours For Life" telethon, 28
Skinner, E. M., 48
Skozen, Al, 28
Small Wind Band, 83
Smith, Jane, 15

  Roger, 124
Smithsonian Institute, 35
Society for the Performing Arts, 29, 121, 122–123
"Soiree Musical," 52
"Soiree on the Swanee," 20, 25, 34, 120, 123, 125
Sotheby's, 67
SPA Angels, 29, 121, 123
SPCA, 72
Sportsmania, 63–66, 100
Stafford, Diane, 89
Staley, Earl, 90
Stardust, 7
Star of Hope recovery centers, 40
"Stars of Texas Gala," 42–44
Steele, Dayna, 144
Stehlin, Dr. John, 16, 38, 72, 73
Stehlin Foundation for Cancer Research, 1, 16, 38, 72–73, 85, 125
Steinem, Gloria, 42–44
"Step Back In Time, A," 23–24, 31, 103, 114
Stern, David, 18
Stevens, Roger, 50
Stevenson, Ben, 38
Stevens and Pruett Humane Ranch, 72
Strake, George, 61
Strange, Don, 30, 114
Strauss, Annette, 23
Stritch, Billy, 36
Studebakers, 141
Sudden Impact, 47
Surls, James, 90
Sween, Trudy, 25, 94
Swit, Loretta, 43

T
T. H. Rogers school, 31, 41–42, 55
TACA, 50
Taft Architects, 114

Tallchief, Maria, 61
Tanenbaum, Dick, 134
  Glenna, 134
Taylor, Elizabeth, 87
Tellez, Tom, 18
Texas A&M University, 36
Texas Chamber Orchestra, 52
Texas Children's Hospital, 2, 28
Texas Christian University, 46
Texas Governor's Inaugural Ball,
  126
Texas Medical Center, 2, 128
Texas Medical Center Hospice, 88
Texas Monthly, 88, 115
Texas Neurofibromatosis Founda-
  tion, 24, 85, 104, 134, 135
Texas Renaissance Festival, 59
Thanksgiving Day Parade, 26
Theater Under the Stars, 19
This is NF, 84
Thomas, Charlie, 18
  Danny, 6
  Kittsie, 18
  Marlo, 43
Thomas Street Center, 79, 107–108
Thompson, Frances Merritt, 82–83
Thwing, Dale, 114
Tocqueville, Alexis de, 45
Tomjohnavich, Rudy, 18
Tony's Restaurant, 63, 86, 120
Transco, 43
Transco Tower, 96, 121–122
Trapani, Lisa, 53
Tree, Marietta, 74
"Tribute to Excellence," 16–18, 58
Tucker, Sophie, 6
Turner, Lisa, 44

U
United Cerebral Palsy, 55, 57, 96
United Cerebral Palsy Center, 62
United Cerebral Palsy Starathon
  '90, 19, 25–26, 61–66, 87,
  100, 132

University of Houston, 16–18, 58,
  103
University of Houston Architec-
  tural School, 124
University of Houston Conrad
  Hilton Inn, 17
University of Texas at San Anto-
  nio Madrigal Group, 67
Urban Animals, 103, 114
USO, 47–49

V
Vaughn, Natt, 113
Vener, Ellis, 88
Veneto, Bartolommeo, 86
Viens, Red, 11
Villa Fontana, 81
Virginia Slims, 74
Volkswagen of America, 43
Volunteers of America, 39–40,
  143, 145, 148
Von Furstenberg, Prince Egon, 86

W
Waldrep, Kent, 46–47
Ward, Dave, 112
Ware, Andre, 18
Warhol, Andy, 118
Warhol Foundation, 118
Wariner, Steve, 112
Warren, David, 59
Warwick Hotel, 55
Watriss, Wendy, 115
Weddington, Sara, 43
Weinstein, Paula, 46
Weiss Gallery, 30
Welch, Louie, 87, 88
Westin Corporation, 104
Westin Oaks, 47
Westin Oaks/Galleria, 135, 138
White, Linda Gayle, 61
  Mark, 51, 61

Whitmire, Kathryn, 33, 36, 47, 82, 84, 107, 123, 145
Whitney Museum, 74
Winkler, Paul, 52
"Women We Admire," 29, 58
Woodward, Joanne, 74
Woolfenden, William E., 35–36
World Headquarters Newsletter, 49
Wortham Center, 18, 19, 31, 103, 113, 118

Y
Yankelovich, Daniel, 13
York, Michael, 112
YWCA, 42

Z
Zadora, Pia, 16, 112
zero–budget philosophy, 23–27, 97
Zindler, Marvin, 63, 71, 113
Zoo Ball, 30